BLACK & BLUE

BLACK & BLUE:

HOW OBAMA AND THE DEMOCRATS ARE BEATING UP THE CONSTITUTION

Alan Gottlieb

Merril Press
Bellevue, Washington

Black & Blue is published by
Merril Press, P.O. Box 1682, Bellevue, WA 98009.
www.merrilpress.com
Phone: 425-454-7009

Distributed to the book trade by
Midpoint Trade Books, 27 W. 20th Street, New York, N.Y. 10011
www.midpointtradebooks.com
Phone: 212-727-0190

Library of Congress Cataloging-in-Publication Data

Gottlieb, Alan M.
    Black & blue : how Obama and the Democrats are beating up the Constitution / Alan Gottlieb.
        p. cm.
    ISBN 978-0-936783-62-8
    1. United States--Politics and government--2009- 2. United States. Constitution. 3. Democratic Party (U.S.) 4. Obama, Barack. I. Title. II. Title: Black and blue.
    JK275.G684 2010
    973.932092--dc22

                                2010033421

Printed in the United States

Dedication

To Ron and Janet Arnold,
who have been there for me
from the Reagan era of "trickle down" economics
to the Obama era of "trickle up" poverty.

Table of Contents

The Rule of Law

It was a fairly routine Tuesday morning at the White House. CNBC correspondent John Harwood sat conducting an interview with President Barack Obama.

In the middle of the conversation, a fly buzzed by. Then it buzzed back.

"Get out of here," the president told the pesky insect.

When it didn't, he waited for the fly to settle, and it landed on his left hand. Obama quickly lashed out with his right hand and whacked it dead. He brushed it off onto the floor.

"Now, where were we?" Obama asked Harwood, unruffled.

Then he added smugly: "That was pretty impressive, wasn't it? I got the sucker."

The YouTube clip of the fly-whacking incident showed up in my email, and I got a chuckle watching it like everybody else.

Then it hit me.

"That's not just an amusing quirk," I realized.

"That's totally symbolic of Barack Obama – and his one-party Congress, too. That's what they're doing to the United States Constitution."

Whacking it dead and brushing it off onto the floor.

"Now, where were we?"

That's a good question to ask ourselves as we slog through the Obama presidency.

We were in a country that honored the rule of law and whacked down politicians who overreached their authority. Now we seem to be in a country that whacks down the rule of law and honors politicians who overreach their authority: we have a president with hitherto unimagined executive power to allocate vast portions of the nation's wealth where he wishes.

We were in a country that actually debated the public policy issues of abortion, taxes, illegal immigration, international trade, and national security. Now we seem to be in a country that brands anyone who stands up against the president's hitherto unimagined executive power as a wacko, or a threat, or a terrorist.

We were in a country that defended free enterprise and respected moneymaking ability. Now we seem to be in a country that destroys free enterprise and despises moneymaking ability: we have a president with hitherto unimagined executive discretion to control, to seize, or to break up the producers of the nation's wealth.

We should have paid attention back when First Lady Michelle Obama was just a senator's wife telling a group of Zanesville, Ohio women at a local day care center, "don't go into corporate America, become social workers or others in the helping industry, not the moneymaking industry."

It wasn't just campaign rhetoric. Her liberal loathing of corporate America's moneymaking machine didn't dim a bit when the financial sector's near-death experience started taking homes and jobs and life savings away from millions of Americans. As First Lady, she said the very same thing to the 2009 graduating class of Washington Math and Science Technical High School in Washington, DC.

It's hard to imagine that her husband, who has hitherto unimagined executive power, doesn't feel the same way.

That goes for Obama Democrats in Congress. Despite their own liberal distaste for corporate America, they rushed with Obama's Treasury Secretary Timothy Geithner to save the "moneymaking industry" when the "mortgage bubble" burst. It wasn't just an epiphany that moneymaking was important, they had something in mind besides "bailout."

Some Wall Street firms with too many subprime mortgage-backed securities, particularly those firms well-stocked with generous election campaign contributors, were judged "too big to fail," even though the market said they weren't.

Nobody in their right mind would buy worthless mortgage paper. So Congress did – they passed TARP, the "Troubled Asset Relief Program" to buy up "toxic assets" (unpaid mortgages) held on bank balance sheets.

Guilt may have played a role, too: a good part of the blame for those "toxic assets" belonged to Congress. A string of liberal banking laws running from the Carter Administration up to the Clinton Administration required banks to give mortgage loans to people who could never pay them back.

Subprime mortgages were the work of subprime policy makers.

Face it, Wall Street's most toxic assets came from toxic laws.

And Obama Democrats in Congress were about to pass more of them.

Like Obama's White House Chief of Staff Rahm Emanuel told a Wall Street Journal reporter, "You never want a serious crisis go to waste. It's an opportunity to do things that you couldn't do before."

Before, they couldn't turn the private sector into the public sector – they couldn't whack down the moneymaking industry and put it under direct government control.

So, while they handed out money – and obligations – to failing financial institutions and troubled auto makers, they also handed out new powers up and down the bureaucracy. They claimed to be helping us build back from a deep and devastating economic crisis.

What they were really doing was building a power structure beyond anything America has ever experienced – along with a deficit beyond anything America has ever experienced.

They were beating the rule of law black and blue.

Now they could whack down and take control of the private sector and turn it into the public sector – the government sector – and claim it would save us from a serious crisis.

They're whacking down everything you can think of, the economy, oil policy, trade agreements, foreign affairs, and domestic policy.

They're whacking down our banks, insurance companies and mortgage companies.

And Treasury Secretary Timothy Geithner was given control.

They're whacking down our auto makers.

And White House "Car Czar" Steven Rattner was given control.

They're whacking down our telecommunications.

And Justice Department anti-trust snoop Christine Varney was given control.

They're whacking down our energy.

And Energy Secretary Steven Chu, global warming zealot, was given control.

They're whacking down our health care.

They're whacking down our gun rights.

They're whacking down talk radio.

They're whacking down our most cherished value:

They're whacking down the rule of law.

Whack. "That was pretty impressive, wasn't it? I got the sucker."

Now, where were we?

We were about to ask if we could have seen it coming. The answer is yes.

When Barack Obama was a senator from Illinois, he gave us a big clue about his regard for the rule of law. Steven G. Calabresi, cofounder of the Federalist Society and a professor of law at Northwestern University, warned us in the pages of the *Wall Street Journal*:

Speaking in July 2007 at a conference of Planned Parenthood, he said: "[W]e need somebody who's got the heart, the empathy, to recognize what it's like to be a young teenage mom. The empathy to understand what it's like to be poor, or African-American, or gay, or disabled, or old. And that's the criteria by which I'm going to be selecting my judges."

On this view, plaintiffs should usually win against defendants in civil cases; criminals in cases against the police; consumers, employees and stockholders in suits brought against corporations; and citizens in suits brought against the government. Empathy, not justice, ought to be the mission of the federal courts, and the redistribution of wealth should be their mantra.

Obama voted against the confirmation of Chief Justice John Roberts, saying that deciding "truly difficult cases" should involve "one's deepest values, one's core concerns, one's broader perspectives on how the world works, and the depth and breadth of one's empathy."

Empathy? He said the same thing when he nominated Federal Appeals Court Judge Sonia Sotomayor to the United States Supreme Court.

"We need somebody who's got the heart, the empathy, to recognize what it's like to be a young teenage mom. The empathy to understand what it's like to be poor, or African-American, or gay, or disabled, or old."

Yeah, yeah, we heard you the first time.

That goes against everything in American jurisprudence.

Just the other day I saw an article about a federal judge in Seattle who gave instructions to jurors in a civil rights case that their deliberations "must not be influenced by any personal likes or dislikes, opinions, prejudices or sympathies." That's a direct quote.

Every new federal judge is required by federal law to take an oath of office in which he swears that he will "administer justice without respect to persons, and do equal right to the poor and to the rich."

But Obama goes whack. "I got the sucker."

The "sucker" he whacked was justice.

Obama's Statue of Justice would be peeking under her blindfold and the double-edged sword in her right hand would be pressing down on one side of the scale in her left hand.

We should have asked Senator Obama what "empathy" has to do with judging.

In her Senate confirmation hearing, even Obama's first Supreme Court nominee, Sonia Sotomayor, had to disavow his "empathy" remark.

Should our judges side with whichever party in a courtroom stirs their empathy? What effect would judging on the basis of our emotions do to the rule of law?

It would make us ignore the language and spirit of the Constitution and the legislation that guides a free society.

It would beat the rule of law black and blue.

It was clear from his first address to Congress in early 2009 that President Obama fancies himself the defender of the people, the voice of the grass roots, herald of a new kind of politics from below. Obama's new politics would upset the established lobbyist special-interest order of Washington, he promised.

But a few short months later, during the first summer of his presidency, Obama faced protests from a real grass-roots movement that was not only outraged by his wildly complicated and expensive health care plan, but also furious with his takeover of the financial and automotive sectors of our economy, behavior we might expect from some banana republic dictator.

How did his party and his supporters in "the new politics" handle real protest? They called it a mob – misinformed, misled, irrational, angry, unbalanced, bordering on racist, just plain wrong. All this while Obama's staff , executive office, and cabinet were cutting backroom deals with every manner of health care special interest – from drug companies to auto unions to doctors – quietly exchanging off-the-record favors worth billions.

We know Barack Obama is left of center, but how far left? Is he just another partisan New Deal Democrat pushing the same old big government tax and spend agenda? It's clear that he believes that our social ills can be solved by bigger government taxing producers more heavily and re-distributing their money to those who do not produce.

But what about individual rights, like the civil liberties in the Bill of Rights, and later legislation like the secret ballot? Does Obama look forward to rewriting the Constitution, like Hugo Chavez did in Venezuela, to create the Socialist States of America – or worse?

And what about those thirty or more "czars" who are "advising" on major projects and budgets throughout Obama's administration?   A few advisors have been part of most administrations since the early 20th Century, but not a few dozen. Why is Obama building up such a huge cadre of appointed bureaucrats without Senate confirmation who are answerable only to him and not to Congress?

I'm certainly not the only one asking such questions. Many worry what Obama will do to the constitutional republic he has sworn to "preserve, protect and defend" – maybe there's something significant in the awkward fact that he had to take the oath of office three times before he got it word perfect.

Will Obama bring America to her knees through a policy of "managed decline," bowing to international opinion, and leaving our great nation a second-rate country beneath the European Union, China and India?

Will he listen to green extremists who advise him to keep fuel prices high in order to immobilize Americans into powerlessness?

Will he take twenty-five percent of our farmland out of production to satisfy those same environmentalist demands for sprawling windmill farms and vast solar arrays, causing increased food prices and worldwide food shortages?

Will he listen to the most radical environmental leaders who want to use the Endangered Species Act as a "habitat-control" law that is really a "land-control" program to confiscate private property?

Will he allow the Federal Communications Commission to impose the Fairness Doctrine on radio talk shows to silence opposition from wildly popular hosts like Rush Limbaugh and force them aside with weak comedians like Al Franken and his dismal Air America Radio flop that left him with no alternative but to become a U.S. Senator?

Will he violate the secret ballot with union-boss demands for card check instead?

Will he allow felons and illegal immigrants to vote in order to keep left-wing politicians in office forever?

Will he stack the Supreme Court with liberal justices who will repudiate the Second Amendment as a personal right to keep and bear arms?

Will he try to revive the Global Poverty Act of 2007 and spend an additional hundred-billion dollars a year on humanitarian aid to other countries while Americans go jobless at home?

Will he keep peeling away America's military power like cancelling the F-14 fighter plane until our military is so weak it cannot defend our shores?

Will he try to give every leftist constituency in his base what they want? And do we have a realistic assessment of what that is?

Can we even guess what more we should be asking about Barack Obama?

Questions. Troubling questions.

Obama's outlook is troubling, because it doesn't fit the American picture of life, liberty and the pursuit of happiness. It doesn't fit our profound respect for the rule of law instead of the rule of charismatic leaders. It doesn't fit our history of prosecuting and imprisoning corrupt politicians who thought they were above the law.

Obama knows better. He has a *Juris Doctor* degree from Harvard Law School, *magna cum laude*. He knows that justice does not bend the rule of law because you're "poor, or African-American, or gay, or disabled, or old." He knows that the facts of the case and the evidence make the difference. But he clearly thinks something else that we're not getting.

Obama knows what the Constitution says. He taught courses in constitutional law at the University of Chicago Law School. He caused a flap when he said at a March 30, 2007, fundraiser, "I was a constitutional law professor, which means unlike the current president [George W. Bush] I actually respect the Constitution."

Republicans and rival presidential candidate Hillary Rodham Clinton jumped all over him for calling himself a "professor," when he was only a Senior Lecturer, but the University of Chicago Law School backed him up in a public statement: "Senior Lecturers are considered to be members of the Law School faculty and are regarded as professors, although not full-time or tenure-track." They had even invited him to join the faculty as a tenure-track professor, but he declined in favor of political office.

How can a man with such a strong legal background be so willing – as the President of the United States (the POTUS in White House-speak) – to overreach the rule of law?

Sure, he's an appealing nice guy – even Osama bin Laden likes him because of the 2009 speech he gave in Cairo kissing up to Muslims.

But that doesn't mean he can't do irreparable harm.

What are we missing?

In a word, Power.

The ability to make others do what you want whether they want to or not.

That's another part of Barack Obama's background, one that hasn't been probed enough.

Maybe we missed it because Americans have always been suspicious of power – a legacy of 1776, the Revolutionary War against England's King George III, the man Thomas Jefferson and the other Founders called a tyrant. They felt it so keenly that the first Independence Day celebration had no Fourth of July fireworks, just mock-funerals for Tyrant King George!

The Founders separated our government into three independent branches, the Executive, the Legislative, and the Judiciary, for a good reason: they didn't trust concentrated power.

We don't either.

Nobody gets all the marbles. That's the American way.

What many of us see is Barack Obama trying to get all the marbles – government control of finance, auto makers, energy, health care, private property, water rights, gun rights, and who knows what else with all the "czars" he's appointed?

That scares a lot of us, regardless of party politics. Obama and his Obama Democrats are giving themselves powers so massive that Blue Dog Democrats have become a sizeable faction – ones that don't go along with the Obama power agenda.

So it's time to probe that power agenda, and see if we can find a way to stop the rule of law from being whacked and brushed off onto the floor.

It's time to look into Barack Obama, the power-seeker.

Who is this guy?

And where did he get power hunger?

Who Is This Guy?

"It's all about power."

That's what Ryan Lizza told *PBS Frontline* about Barack Obama's life history.

Lizza has covered Obama for more than four years as Washington correspondent for *The New Yorker*. He thinks it first began to show when Obama decided to leave his Chicago community organizing job and apply to Harvard Law School.

"Before Obama went off to Harvard, he said to some of his community-organizing buddies he needed that credential, that Harvard Law degree, to access the corridors of power and to have that credential because he wasn't going to get that as a community organizer in Chicago."

It's all about power.

Somehow, in the middle of his personal mission to help Chicago's black community, Barack Obama decided that access to the corridors of power was more important.

And this is one of the great questions about Obama: how did that happen?

Was it there all along? Or did he change once he had been trained in community organizing?

Lizza offers this tantalizing clue: "When people start community organizing, and they learn that the whole ethos of the community organizer is to understand power, this can sound sort of negative. In fact, in the seminars that Obama went through, this was drilled into his head: Don't think of power as a negative thing. Power is the only thing that changes anything."

That sounds like Gordon Gekko in the 1987 movie *Wall Street*, who famously said, "Greed is good."

But in Obama's liberal Chicago, it was "Power is good."

Whack!

Okay, let's assume there's something to this. My bet is that the affable young Obama came equipped with a natural dose of personal ambition – not with some secret flaw (besides smoking cigarettes, which friends say he still may not have quit, and a politician's expertise at telling lies) – and he really did develop into a power-seeker from his experience as a Chicago community organizer.

That's not making excuses for him. Quite the opposite. It's a warning. Obama's training as a community organizer – which is a lot more sinister than just dishing up dinner for the poor in some soup kitchen – honed that ambitious but genial personality into a cold-blooded, calculating, hard-nosed, and resolute *weapon*, an iron fist in a velvet glove.

And it put him in contact not only with some of Chicago's finest minority leaders, but also a whole lot of its unsavory characters:

• Convicted felon Tony Rezko, restaurateur and developer who financed Obama's Chicago home...

• Bill Ayers, revolutionary bomber and co-founder of the 1970s' violent Weather Underground...

• and some future voter-fraud ACORN denizens.

People can't see the incipient autocrat lurking inside Obama's too-normal, smooth-talking, it's-all-so-reasonable, media-protected, velvet glove.

But the iron fist is there.

Just think of the dustup about Obama's buddy, prickly Harvard Professor Henry Louis Gates, and the President calling the Cambridge cop who busted him for breaking into his own home "stupid."

Whack!

Obama had to hold a White House beer fest to tamp that one down.

Nevertheless, because it's human nature to read more into a situation than is really there, it's worth looking into Obama's life story to see whether he is what he says he is, or whether there is some psychological defect driving him.

To start with, Obama had a weird childhood, which might have traumatized him into predatory power hunger – but, frankly, although it had its lumps, it wasn't all that tough.

By the way, Obama's mother, Stanley Ann Dunham, went to upscale Mercer Island High School near Seattle, Washington – about five miles from my home – where she was known as a feisty, agnostic, non-conformist with a man's first name (her father's, who had desperately wanted a son).

The official story is that Barack Hussein Obama (Junior, his father had the same name) was born in 1961 in Hawaii (no, the birth certificate flap won't ever die). He had a black father from Kenya and a white mother from Kansas who met in a Russian language class at the University of Hawaii.

He was 25, she was 18.

Barack went by "Barry" to fit in with the Americans, and Stanley Ann dropped her father's name and went by "Ann" to avoid the inevitable question.

They married in early 1961, Barack Junior arrived later the same year, and they divorced when the boy was three – after Ann Dunham Obama discovered that Barack Senior already had a wife named Kezia and a child (or two) back in Kenya and no divorce.

Anyway, a year earlier, the father had jumped at the offer of a graduate economics scholarship at the more prestigious Harvard University in Massachusetts, abandoning Ann and little Barack in Hawaii.

Obama has said so many different things about his father that it's hard to know what's true, but none of it seems to have made him power-hungry. We have independent reports that his father was born into a Muslim family, but wasn't religious. Barack Senior was such a dashing womanizer his relatives in

Kenya aren't sure how many children he fathered – "probably six," said one uncle, but others say eight. We know that he was a dedicated socialist, as most educated Africans were as the colonial era came to a close.

After earning a master's degree at Harvard, Obama Senior returned to Kenya (with Ruth Nidesand, a well-off new white American wife) and worked first for an oil company and later for Jomo Kenyatta's socialist government, advancing to the powerful position of senior economist in the Ministry of Finance.

In 1971, Obama Senior visited Obama Junior for a month in Hawaii – the only time the two met after the father abandoned the son. It was not a smooth visit – the father's career in Kenya was faltering, and it showed in his behavior, constantly bossing the kid around and making himself a general annoyance.

Back in Kenya, Obama Senior's personal abrasiveness and a nasty outbreak of tribal political violence cost him his fine job. Obama was Luo, Kenyatta was Kikuyu, and Obama not only criticized Kenyatta in print for giving the best jobs to unqualified Kikuyu men (throwing his Harvard education around), but also testified at the 1969 trial of a Kikuyu suspect in the assassination of his high-ranking Luo political mentor, Tom Mboya – Obama had been at the scene shortly before Mboya was shot to death. That unwise testimony got him sidelined into the tourism ministry for a while, but in the waning years of the Kenyatta administration, he was reinstated at the finance ministry in a lower position. He fell into alcoholism and despair. He died in a car crash while driving drunk in Nairobi in 1982 at the age of 46.

The father's main legacy to his son was bitterness over being deserted and confusion about his race – was he white or black or just half-and-half? It's a ridiculous stretch to imagine that Barack Senior's graduate study of economics at Harvard later drove Barack Junior to get a degree from Harvard Law School so he too could enter the corridors of power like his socialist Dad. His father's fate was more a cautionary tale than a prod to power.

It's less of a stretch to ask whether being abandoned by his father left such deep emotional scars on the young Obama that he obsessively sought fame and power to salve a wounded ego.

Nice psychobabble theory, but all accounts of his youth by those who knew him say he was only an ordinary, easy-going kid, doing what everybody else did, not a smoldering powder keg brooding over personal hurts and plotting vengeance on an uncaring world.

Obama's mother remarried in 1965, this time to an Indonesian fellow student, Lolo Soetoro – Muslim, like Barack Senior – who was called to come back home by his government. So the boy lived in Jakarta from age 6 to 10. There he attended a Catholic school first and later a Muslim public school – and no, the Muslim school wasn't run by Al-Qaeda and the Catholic school wasn't run by the Inquisition. And yes, Obama was enrolled in both schools as "Barry Soetoro" and his religion was listed in both as Islam, like his step-father. He learned to recite from the Koran – and he learned the Our Father from the Catholics.

Some critics have made much of Obama's loyalty to Islam – and he certainly has a lot of Muslim friends, many of whom applaud his unsympathetic treatment of Israel in favor of the Palestinian cause. But I think that's his internationalist politics and his habit of collecting a wide spectrum of personal contacts, not his religious beliefs, at work. His personal religious faith appears to have been inspired more by pragmatic opportunism than by spirituality, as we shall see.

Obama says that his sojourn in Jakarta showed him racism and abject poverty for the first time – and friends from the time say it's true that he got into fights at school, but it was more because he insisted on tagging along with the big kids (they once threw him into a swamp for pestering them) than about his being black, and he lived not in poverty, but well-off in a nice red-tile roofed brick home in a decent neighborhood.

The years in Jakarta also gave him a half-sister, Maya Soetoro, born to Lolo and Ann in 1970.

Muslim or not, it doesn't look like Obama had been indoctrinated into power-hunger by the age of ten.

But in 1971, his mother sent him back to school in Honolulu to live with her mother and father, Madelyn and Stanley Dunham – Tutu (Hawaiian for grandmother) and Gramps. They put him in Punahou School, the biggest and one of the best private college prep schools in America ($16,675 a year in 2009). It took Stanley's influence with a Punahou graduate just to get the kid on the waiting list.

Obama claims he suffered as a "misfit" at Punahou, but classmates recall him as a fairly normal prep school kid just like them – intelligent beyond his years but not overly intellectual, okay but not stellar grades (B-minus average), resentful of Punahou's snotty rich cliques of the pineapple Doles and the Waikiki developers' kids, while at the same time enjoying his cool status as a student in Hawaii's most elite school – but not above dishing up ice cream at a Baskin and Robbins store as his first job during high school.

His main oddity was that he sang in the choir and joined Ka Wai Ola, the school's literary journal. Thus, he learned to enunciate lyrical phrases precisely and compose a graceful compound-complex English sentence by his mid-teens. His extensive vocabulary, exceptional writing skills, and his sonorous speaking style bear the stamp of Punahou.

But classmates don't remember Obama as an angry black kid who stayed up nights reading angry African-American authors and smoking dope to push racial anguish from his mind, as Obama has made himself out to be. Not that he didn't smoke dope, he did, but as fun with his school buddies. His 1979 Punahou *Ohauan* senior yearbook entry thanked his grandparents and his "Choom Gang" – "chooming" is Hawaiian slang for smoking marijuana. And he was nicknamed "Barry O'Bomber" for nailing long shots on Punahou's Buff'n'Blue varsity basketball team. Basketball remained an important personal outlet beyond prep school – his left-handed double pump shot let him show off a little at pickup games in college and after.

In 1972, Barack's mother left her second husband and moved back to Honolulu with Maya, where she returned to the university for an anthropology degree. They lived with Barry in a small apartment near Punahou until he was 13, when Ann and Maya returned to Indonesia so the mother could complete fieldwork for her master's degree.

Abandoned again – but this time it was his decision to stay in Hawaii, not his mother's. He didn't want to leave the comfortable Dunham life and he liked his friends at Punahou. According to a *Chicago Tribune* story titled, "The not-so-simple story of Barack Obama's youth," Obama's 1995 memoir, *Dreams from My Father*, contained a web of fuzzy memories, exaggerated claims, and flat lies ("crap," according to one of the students who knew him, "bull" according to another, who said their long buddy talks were about his loneliness for his parents, not about race).

And that "loneliness" itself may be a ruse – why didn't he just go with Mama and Sis? One of literature's best judges of political character, Peter Kaplan, fifteen-year veteran editor of the power publication, the *New York Observer*, said in 2007 that Obama was great because he is cold. "And Jack Kennedy was cold, too."

Kaplan, and not a few other individuals, have said that people don't fully register emotionally in Obama's consciousness, they're expendable, he's arrogant, lacks empathy. One of the first episodes in his book's chapter on entering Punahou describes how he physically pushed a black girl named "Coretta" away from him because the white kids taunted him for having a "girl friend." Obama, of course, feels remorse that he "was tried and found wanting."

Maybe he was just a ten-year-old kid who wanted to get in good with the right crowd – and stay in comfy, rich Punahou.

The Dunham grandparents took Obama back into their apartment and, at significant financial sacrifice, continued seeing to it that he was raised middle-class white. Gramps, Stanley Dunham, had been born in conservative Wichita, and his ancestry went back to English settlers in Massachusetts in 1640.

He was a furniture salesman, had a zest for life, tended to tall tales, and gravitated toward intelligent, quirky friends, including a black man, Frank Marshall Davis – a genuine member of the Communist Party USA (CPUSA). Gramps introduced the two, and Obama grew close to Davis, supposedly learning Marxist ideology in academic detail – 2004 U.S. Senate opponent, Republican Alan Keyes, made that allegation, and Obama admits attending "socialist meetings" with Davis.

But 17-year-old Obama a "Marxist"? That sounds overblown to me – Marx wrote some fifty volumes of studies, essays and newspaper columns, which even devoted communists have never read – but it's undoubtedly significant. It means that Obama got his first exposure to some version of socialism from Davis while still attending Punahaou – probably the propagandistic "class struggle for the oppressed underdog" and "workers of the world unite" sizzle, not the academic "dialectical materialism" and "historical materialism" steak (and no, Obama won't talk about that). I don't think Davis made Obama a high school socialist, but he certainly gave the boy a foundation to build on in college, and prompted his later feeling for socialist ideas.

And the Dunhams raised him ambitious – Madelyn was a Bank of Hawaii vice-president when they took him in, one of the first women to hold such a high banking office, and all the more remarkable because *haole* ("foreigners," meaning whites) were the despised minority in Hawaii at the time. For example, the last day of school before summer was traditionally known as Kill Haole Day. On Kill Haole Day, school children of Hawaiian ancestry harassed, and sometimes assaulted, white children. Madelyn felt the sting of being on the receiving end of such racism, but feared black men because of a stalking incident.

Obama learned that his Tutu Madelyn had disapproved of her daughter's marriage to his father, and he held it against her – his mother Ann had always cultivated pride in his African heritage. When Ann Dunham married Obama Senior, such inter-racial marriages were a felony – *miscegenation* – in half the states, although Hawaii never enacted such a law. Obama Junior eventually came to terms with his grandmother. And Obama finished Punahou (with half a dozen other black kids) without once being harassed on Kill Haole Day.

Then came college.

Barack (he used his formal name in college because it sounded cooler and more defiant than "Barry") remained close to the Dunhams, even though they didn't like him using "Barack." He also accepted their generosity through two years of Occidental College in Los Angeles, and two years at hot-shot Columbia University in New York City, where he earned a B.A. degree in 1983 (political science with a specialization in international affairs, but without honors).

Obama has said little about Occidental. He wrote in his 1995 memoir, *Dreams from My Father*, that he partied and got high as a form of rebellion. And he got a jolt about race: once he and his buddies were joking about the Mexican cleaning woman's forlorn reaction to the mess they'd made at a party, and a fellow black student, a young Chicago woman, snapped Obama back to reality with a bitter rebuke: "You think that's funny? That could have been my grandmother, you know. She had to clean up behind people for most of her life."

We know he went to Occidental on a full scholarship for his first year, but had to take out more than $20,000 in student loans for the second. He went home to Hawaii the summer after his freshman year and worked selling Island trinkets in a gift shop.

One of his roommates at Occidental, Vinai Thummalapally, a native of India, remembers the 19-year-old Obama as wanting to go into public service. He recalls Obama saying. "I want to write and help people who are disadvantaged." Meaning he never felt disadvantaged himself.

Obama spent the summer after his sophomore year back in Hawaii making sandwiches at a deli counter. That's pretty much all we know about Occidental.

His time at Columbia is a little more detailed.

A photo survives of Obama and his Gramps and Tutu (sometimes he just called her Tut – pronounced "toot."), smiling together on a park bench at Columbia. The Dunhams were still on close terms with their grandson and still helping pay the bills, although Barack worked during the school year as a telemarketer in midtown Manhattan selling *New York Times* subscriptions over the phone, wearing a headset.

Columbia is a respected Ivy League school that's hard to get into. Its reputation for political science and international affairs is impeccable: The faculty in the early 1980s included Zbigniew Brzezinski, the former national security adviser, and Zalmay Khalilzad, former American ambassador to the United Nations.

Columbia's elite status has led to speculation that Obama may have gotten a free ride from affirmative action programs. We know that Obama worked a summer job while at Columbia for a private company that held a contract to process health records of New York City employees – his first job that didn't have customer contact. Obama has claimed he paid for Columbia with student loans, but his educational records are all sealed, so we don't know.

What else *do* we know about his Columbia years?

As far as outlook, Columbia certainly equipped Obama with the Ivy League's usual liberal slant – the Keynesian welfare state, the habit of saying "progressive" when you mean "socialist," and a distinct distaste for corporate America. And he *had* read all the angry black literature of the time, from Frantz Fanon and W.E.B. DuBois through Stokely Carmichael to Malcolm X. By then, he *did* have an obsession with race, mostly trying hard to be black when he didn't have the proper background.

At Columbia he lived off-campus in cheap apartments, got a taste of the Big Apple's seedier side (north of gentrification, he likes to say), supposedly became involved with the Black Students Organization and participated in anti-apartheid activities, but the *New York Times* said that several well-known student leaders did not recall his involvement. It's probably a false claim, i.e., he's lying again.

When Columbia handed Obama his political science diploma in 1983, it didn't fire him up to rush into the corridors of power.

Obama wrote in *Dreams from My Father*, "In 1983 I decided to become a community organizer... Change won't come from the top. Change will come from a mobilized grass roots. That's what I'll do. I'll organize black folks. At the grass roots. For change."

That's probably just another charming bit of after-the-fact embellishment, since he stayed in New York after graduation for two more years not being a community organizer.

Obama claims he spent those two years searching for work as a community organizer, but couldn't find any – an unlikely story because many Columbia faculty members and student leaders could easily have directed him to well-known hotbeds like the Tides Foundation in San Francisco and Midwest Academy in Chicago.

The actual record isn't so lofty. During 1984, he worked at Business International Corporation, an advisory firm for Americans doing business abroad. His job there was to research and write for a reference service called Financing Foreign Operations, along with writing for the company's newsletter, *Business International Money Report*.

After about a year, he was hired by the New York Public Interest Research Group (NYPIRG), a Ralph Nader-inspired far-left student political group pushing consumer, environmental and government reform. He became a full-time student coordinator at City College in Harlem, paid slightly less than $10,000 a year to recruit members and mobilize volunteers on bread-and-butter issues like mass transit, higher education, tuition and financial aid. Obama claims he was just teaching college kids to recycle, but his boss remembers it as being a lot more political.

Eileen Hershenov, who oversaw Obama's work for NYPIRG, told the *New York Times* that the job required winning over students on the political left, as well as students on the right and those who were not active at all. Recycling lessons don't require that kind of talent.

"You needed somebody — and here was where Barack was a star — who could make the case to students across the political spectrum."

So, by 1985, Obama was still treading water. When you know the details, you still don't see much evidence of power-lust.

Coincidentally, Obama worked with NYPIRG while founding director Donald K. Ross was still there. Ross had been tapped to leave NYPIRG and take over as executive director of the ultra-liberal Rockefeller Family Fund. Ross is one of the Left's most astute political strategists when it comes to mobilizing grass-roots.

I wouldn't be at all surprised if Ross and Hershenov had whipped Obama into shape as a budding left-wing win-at-any-cost tactician before his Chicago experience.

We have reason to believe they did, because United States PIRG boss Gene Karpinski met Obama in Boston during the 2004 Democratic convention that made him the party's rising star. Karpinski introduced himself, and recalls Obama telling him, "I used to be a PIRG guy. You guys trained me well."

I'll bet.

Okay, so far all we see is some youthful bumbling that Obama had to dress up or cover up later, but no deep-seated psychological flaws beyond lying, which is not that uncommon among politicians.

Where did he get his power hunger?

Next stop, Chicago and community organizing.

So now we need to ask, what happened in Chicago?

What do community organizers actually do? How do they do it? What was in those seminars that Obama took?

And, most of all, why Chicago?

Chicago and Alinsky

Consider the place and the time.

It was 1985.

Chicago was the capital of Black America. Louis Farrakhan had his Nation of Islam headquarters there. Jesse Jackson had his headquarters there. Harold Washington was the city's first black mayor.

Chicago was also the nation's unemployment capital. Once the largest steel-producer and second-largest industrial region, its mills and plants had closed for good. Unemployment wrecked the minority-filled South Side, leaving drugs, gangs, crime and teen pregnancy as the major occupations. Demoralized South Siders needed someone to help take back their streets, restore their dignity and find new sources of employment.

Barack Obama was ready to tackle some of the psychological demons he claimed to harbor: his search for race, for the black half of him that lay embarrassingly undeveloped within; his vagabond Hawaii-Indonesia-Los Angeles-New York life, always bouncing someplace else. The half-white wanderer was ready to put down some roots, to gain a sense of place and permanence he had never known, and to live in a predominantly black community for the first time in his life. And he dreamed about becoming a writer, maybe turn out a good novel.

But none of that mattered.

Barack Obama didn't pick Chicago.

Chicago picked him.

Gerald S. Kellman, a veteran Chicago community organizer, quietly incorporated the Calumet Community Religious Conference in June of 1983 as the control center of a new project to manipulate the diverse black churches of Chicago's South Side into a coherent agent of social change.

Kellman called his proposed church alliance the Developing Communities Project (DCP). He and associates Mike Kruglik and former priest Greg Galluzo of the Gamaliel Foundation needed someone sharp – and African-American – as a credible persuader of black ministers and as lead organizer.

Kellman, Kruglik and Galluzo – three white guys, two of them Jewish – would have no chance getting the DCP off the ground alone in the mostly black South Side.

Kellman began his executive search with an ad in newspapers across the country, including *The New York Times.*

> Help Wanted: Minority community organizer in Chicago. Leadership ability essential. Degree preferred. Will train.

If Kellman hadn't put that ad in the New York paper, I doubt that anybody would know Barack Obama's name today.

The 24-year-old Columbia graduate submitted a sparkling resume and an excited Kellman came to New York to interview him – that's how important an Ivy League kid was to his devious plan.

They met at a coffee shop on Lexington Avenue, and Obama did some of the interviewing himself, wanting to know exactly how he would be trained and what he would be expected to do. He didn't have a clue what community organizers did. But he was sharp – and African-American (enough, anyway). He got the job and moved to Chicago.

Chicago is the right place to learn community organizing: it was invented there.

Obama took 160 pages of his memoir talking about his three years of community organizing, but said nothing about its inventor, who is best known as the author of a 1971 book called *Rules for Radicals*, which begins:

What follows is for those who want to change the world from what it is to what they believe it should be. *The Prince* was written by Machiavelli for the Haves on how to hold power. *Rules for Radicals* is written for the Have-Nots on how to take it away.

In this book we are concerned with how to create mass organizations to seize power and give it to the people; to realize the dream of equality, justice, peace, cooperation, equal and full opportunities for education, full and useful employment, health and the creation of those circumstances in which man can have the chance to live by values that give meaning to life. We are talking about a mass power organization which will change the world into a place where all men and women walk erect, in the spirit of that credo of the Spanish Civil War, "Better to die on your feet than to live on your knees." This means revolution.

Okay, that's a little long-winded, but we get it. We can see why Obama didn't want to talk about it.

That, not coincidentally, is the skeleton key to Obama's campaign slogan, *"Change."* It wasn't just getting rid of the George Bush legacy. The writer of Obama's basic training manual taught: *Change* is taking power away from those who have it and giving it to those who don't.

That's a blunt way to say, "redistribution of wealth," or "class warfare," or "government control." Revolution.

Whack!

The writer of that manual was a brash South Sider named Saul David Alinsky, born in 1909 to Russian-Jewish immigrants. Saul Alinsky grew up in a neighborhood he later called "a cesspool of hate: the Poles, Slovaks, Germans, Negroes, Mexicans and Lithuanians all hated each other and all of them hated the Irish, who returned the sentiment in spades."

It was a seething world of Have-Nots fighting each other – community *dis*organizing.

But it made Alinsky a standup fighter. One of his favorite quotes came from Rabbi Hillel (*circa* 70 BCE), "Where there are no men, be thou a man."

And it made Alinsky a realist. He taught: "It is necessary to begin where the world is if we are going to change it to what we think it should be."

And it made Alinsky a radical. Another of his favorite quotes was the famous Thomas Paine tirade, "Let them call me rebel and welcome. I feel no concern from it; but I should suffer the misery of devils, were I to make a whore of my soul."

Alinsky felt no concern over his radicalism, teaching: "The building of many mass power organizations to merge into a national popular power force cannot come without many organizers." He taught those many organizers "how the Have-Nots can take power from the Haves," with the vision of "a future where the means of production will be owned by all of the people instead of just a comparative handful."

Okay, we get it, we get it.

That should ring a few bells about President Obama's election campaign and his administration's programs.

Now, what about the writer of Obama's training manual? Tough and smart, the young Alinsky worked his way through the University of Chicago and, upon graduation with a degree in sociology, was awarded an unsolicited doctoral fellowship in criminology for reasons he never understood – he'd never even taken a class in the subject.

Not one to pass up a windfall, Alinsky accepted the fellowship. If he had to write a Ph.D. dissertation in criminology, he figured he had to know some criminals. He picked uptown professionals: the Al Capone mob.

He ingratiated himself by haunting known hangouts and chatting up some mid-level thugs who thought it was cute to be studied by an ivory-tower university kid with some street smarts. Alinsky was taken under the wing of Frank Nitti, "the Enforcer," Capone's number two man, who showed him all their gin mills, whorehouses, and bookie operations.

Alinsky didn't finish his Ph.D., but took criminologist posts in Joliet State Prison and the Institute for Juvenile Research. That was going nowhere, so he switched careers to union organizing with the C.I.O. (Congress of Industrial Organizations), getting to be good friends with radical labor boss John L. Lewis.

It was labor organizing that gave Alinsky the big idea that attracted Obama: apply the labor organizing concept to communities. But it didn't just pop into his head full-blown.

The concept was easy: in industries, recruit your workers with one-on-one pump-up sessions about their self-interest – Alinsky said self-interest is the only principle around which to organize people – get your recruits organized, then lead them to the bosses and make collective demands for their self interest.

Doing it was hard: in communities, neighborhoods were too big for one organizer to reach everybody one-on-one, self-interest wasn't defined by a job, and residents didn't know where to present their demands.

Saul Alinsky changed all that during the Great Depression.

Alinsky, the mob-connected criminologist labor organizer, made a name for himself in 1939 by co-founding the Back of the Yards Neighborhood Council (BYNC) in Chicago's South Side.

The "Yards" were the rough Union Stock Yards and vast railroad switching yards that socialist writer Upton Sinclair wrote about in his 1906 book, *The Jungle*.

The "Back of the Yards" was the slum neighborhood of clapboard cottages and two-story tenements where the workers lived.

The BYNC still exists, but its website doesn't mention that Alinsky actually founded it as the Packinghouse Workers Union, organizing Chicago's meatpacking industry. Alinsky was still doing his C.I.O. work.

In reality, Alinsky's community organizing morphed out of his union organizing by circumstance: at the time, the Back of the Yards was still the largely Eastern European neighborhood – Czechs, Lithuanians, Slovaks, and Poles – that Alinsky later described as a "cesspool of hate." Each ethnic enclave had its own church and school. And each was Catholic.

Alinsky wasn't stupid. He went to Bishop Bernard Sheil of the Chicago Catholic Diocese, one of the most left-leaning in the nation at the time, because he knew that without the churches, he would fail.

He also went to Joseph Meegan, superintendent of Davis Square Park, with its famous "fieldhouse," actually an elaborate community center (it even had a swimming pool) used by people from all the enclaves. Everybody knew Meegan, and Alinsky knew that without a widely trusted colleague, he would fail.

Together they organized the Back of the Yards Neighborhood Council with 185 delegate organizations – residents, business owners, churches, parks, schools, and social clubs. Their motto was "We the people will work out our own destiny."

That's all very sweetness and light, like Obama made it sound in his book, but in reality it was an angry, bare-knuckles, confrontational, anti-establishment political machine fighting the packinghouses and government to push the Council's own self interest – to take power from the Haves and give it to the Have-Nots.

They researched power flows, like gathering facts and drawing charts of which corporations gave money to the mayor. They had targets and they hit them hard by jamming meetings with hecklers who humiliated local officials, like Benjamin Willis of Chicago's public school system in the 1960s, accusing him of perpetuating segregation by not sending black kids to white schools and for making space in overcrowded South Side schools using mobile classrooms that Alinsky dubbed "Willis Wagons." Alinsky's Fourth Rule for Radicals is: *Ridicule is man's most potent weapon.*

Alinsky's council ran ferocious campaigns against businesses, always attacking a person, not an abstract idea like segregation or a general institution like a corporation. "It is not possible to generate the necessary hostility against them," he said.

He held up his radical C.I.O. boss, John L. Lewis, as the perfect model for generating "the necessary hostility." Lewis never attacked General Motors, but always attacked its president, Alfred "Icewater-In-His-Veins" Sloan; never Republic Steel, but its president, "Bloodied Hands" Tom Girdler.

Lewis was the inspiration for Alinsky's Thirteenth Rule for Radicals: *Pick the target, freeze it, personalize it and polarize it.*

But there was more to it. In 1940, Alinsky created the Industrial Areas Foundation to train community organizers and develop strategies to place them all over the country – because he had dreams of "building many mass power organizations to merge into a national popular power force." The revolution. Today it has 57 affiliates in 21 states, Canada, the United Kingdom, and Germany.

When the 24-year-old Barack Obama accepted Gerald Kellman's job offer and moved to Chicago in 1985, Alinsky had been dead for thirteen years, but the new kid on the block took workshops and seminars in Alinsky's philosophy and tactics as if taught by the originator.

Kellman had been personally trained by Alinsky.

Mike Kruglik had been personally trained by Alinsky.

Former Jesuit Greg Galluzo called himself "the Apostle Paul of community organizing:" he never met Alinsky, but was taught by his best trainers.

And the Catholic Church was still supporting Alinsky's followers when Obama got there: the Catholic Campaign for Human Development gave a $40,000 grant to Kellman's Developing Communities Project in 1985 and a $33,000 grant in 1986.

Lizza says Kellman also got $25,000 in foundation money specifically to pay for Obama's salary and expenses – including a beat-up Honda – from Jean Rudd, staff director of the Woods Charitable Fund in Chicago, founded in 1941 by the family of Frank H. Woods, wealthy president of a Nebraska telephone company, and his son, Frank H. Woods, Jr., president of Sahara Coal Company, with mines in far Southern Illinois. Rudd created the Fund's community organizing program, and later figured in Obama's political career.

So Obama lied about his salary: It was $25,000 the first year, which his presidential campaign later verified.

What did they teach him?

Obama was naïve on his first day. Then he looked around.

Lesson One, no classroom needed: He would be living in a little Hyde Park apartment, but working a few miles away with the residents of two failing areas: Altgeld Gardens Housing Projects and the decaying Far South Side Roseland community.

Altgeld was a collection of 1,498 two-story brown-brick row houses spread over 190 acres, built in the industrial South Side in 1945 for returning black World War II veterans. It was one of the first public housing developments in America and looked it, run down and sprawling beside shuttered steel mills, waste dumps and landfills, with the Calumet Expressway on its east boundary and the Calumet River on its west. The federal government had granted it to the Chicago Housing Authority in 1956, which had never given it the funding for proper upkeep.

Roseland had once been a large and flourishing multi-ethnic community, but the vanishing steel mills and the shut-down Pullman plant brought skyrocketing crime rates, gang violence and urban decay. Long time residents and businesses moved away in droves, what locals called "white flight." No one was left but minorities, mostly black. New residents purchased homes with federal subsidies and FHA-backed mortgages. By the mid '80s Roseland had one of the highest repossession rates in the city.

Obama knew that about 97 percent of the people he would be organizing were black. The economy of their inner city community had collapsed, the neighborhoods were shabby, the children were edgy and unrestrained, its schools suffered a 50-percent dropout rate, the jails were bursting with glowering youth, no company would think of locating there, middle-class blacks trickled away from the neighborhoods for the suburbs, and volunteers would be scarce – black mothers nowadays didn't stay home, they split themselves between work, raising children, running a household, and maintaining some semblance of a personal life. The South Side's urban landscape was also littered with the skeletons of previous Alinsky community organizing efforts that had failed.

Lesson Two, in Kellman's office: Many of the people he would be recruiting had bitter memories of such failures and would be reluctant to muster up renewed faith in the process. Most of the ministers whose support would be essential to launching the Developing Communities Project still trusted only traditional approaches to social involvement – charity for poor mothers, soup kitchens for the jobless, gospel missions for those with no place to go, and such. Obama's job would be bringing together churches, block clubs, parent groups and individual volunteers to pay dues, hire organizers, conduct research, develop leadership, hold rallies and education campaigns, and begin drawing up plans on a range of issues including jobs, education, and crime. A tough sell. A *really* tough sell.

It was equal amounts pathetic, terrifying and exciting.

Lesson Three, learned in Galluzo's Gamaliel Foundation (incorporated 1968). Obama's training would be conducted by Gamaliel, which was the formal instruction group that Kellman's Calumet Community Religious Conference had contracted with to manage the Developing Communities Project. Galluzo would be his chief classroom instructor with Kruglik teaching him to work the streets. Obama would have to master classroom materials both theoretical and practical. In addition to Kruglik, he would also have access to experienced academics, including:

- Professor John L. McKnight of Northwestern University, who had served in the Johnson administration as director of the Midwest Office of the U.S. Commission on Civil Rights. McKnight had also known and written about Alinsky – his paper, "Community Organizing in the 80's: Toward a Post-Alinsky Agenda," was published in 1984, shortly before Obama came to Chicago. McKnight was a board member of Gamaliel Foundation and two other Chicago community organizations.

- Professor William Julius Wilson of the University of Chicago, a sociologist who was working on a new study that showed growing urban poverty was not being caused by either contemporary racism or an internalized "culture of poverty" value system, but industrial jobs were vanishing in the global economic restructuring, creating a black underclass unprepared to cope with emerging computer-oriented service sector jobs.

In Training Class: Galluzo's first job in the classroom was to ask why his trainees wanted to organize, and then to slap down their response about wanting to help others with Alinsky's shouted one-word answer: "You want to organize for *power!*"

Gamaliel's trainee manual was filled with chapter headings like "power analysis," "elements of a power organization," "power tactics," and "the path to power."

Galluzo taught, "We are not virtuous by not wanting power. We are really cowards for not wanting power. Power is good and powerlessness is evil."

The second thing Obama learned in class was Alinsky's dictum that self-interest is the only principle around which to organize people. No fuzzy-brained idealists allowed. The Gamaliel trainee manual was emphatic on that point: "Get rid of do-gooders in your church and your organization." They did not get rid of Obama.

In fact, Obama told Lizza in a 2007 interview, "The key to creating successful organizations was making sure people's self-interest was met, and not just basing it on pie-in-the-sky idealism. So there were some basic principles that remained powerful then, and in fact I still believe in."

The next step was Kruglik's: getting Obama good at knocking on a lot of doors. Alinsky groups still keep the labor organizer's one-on-one recruiting tactic, and have elevated "generating the necessary hostility" to the first lesson of Street-Level Community Organizing 101.

"Doing a one-on-one" was essentially a disguised sales pitch to find out what a recruit's goals, dreams, and self-interest were, listening compassionately and paying genuine attention to personal concerns, but actually making them feel so defeated, and so mad at what was thwarting them that they were soon ready to join up, pay their dues, and take action.

As Alinsky said, "Before you can screw your enemy, you have to seduce your friend."

His trainers then sent Obama out on his first "one-on-one" to recruit black church leaders for their new DCP, the Developing Communities Project. It was even harder than Kellman had told him, largely because of Obama's personality. His easy-going but strong manner wasn't like Alinsky's or any other community organizer, and he wasn't like any of the people he was hired to recruit. His background did not include ancestors who were slaves and he did not grow up in an urban ghetto. He did not have the hard edge of most American blacks. He could recite line after line of Shakespeare because he had read all the histories and tragedies in college.

Obama knew instinctively not to mimic Chicago black dialect and to stick with his educated vocabulary and sensitive bass voice – trying to sound like an insider when you're not brands you as a fraud. He was the most articulate person most of the locals had ever met, but had to be careful not to use his gift with language to put others down.

So he had to feel his way, a little at a time.

He prowled the South Side's black churches, mostly Baptist and Pentecostal, talking to dozens of ministers about coping with crime, housing problems, and unemployment, and earning a reputation as that skinny kid with the funny name who kept asking about their self-interest.

In return, the ministers asked him so many questions he couldn't answer that "Let me look into it" became his routine parting words.

Obama soon realized that black church leaders were unwilling to help him organize their parishioners in his new DCP, suspicious that he was just working for Catholics and Jews to make money off the black community. He struggled for months with no results.

He claims that a black minister told him it would be helpful if he belonged to a church – more likely Kellman told him – and, as the official version goes, after hearing a sermon about faith's power to inspire underdogs, he joined the Trinity United Church of Christ congregation of Rev. Jeremiah A. Wright, Jr. – later notorious as the "God Damn America" pastor.

Obama, once he conveniently became a recognized church-going Christian in a recognized black church, began getting different church leaders in the same room to talk about organizing their congregations. He quickly found that seducing your friends was the hardest part of community organizing.

Organizing Roseland congregations and the Altgeld Gardens meant dealing with all kinds of people, hardened men barely clinging to jobs in the dwindling factories, neighborhood shopkeepers, office workers, service organization leaders, teens he played pickup basketball with, medical clinics, beat cops, domestics, housewives with seven kids, unemployed men who had given up looking for work, church matrons who doted on him, gave him cookies to fatten him up, and invited him over to meet their marriageable daughters. He'd never had to deal with reality this gritty.

But in time he learned.

He learned that before you can mobilize your people, you have to get to know them and let them get to know you.

He learned that vanishing jobs meant more women refusing to marry the fathers of their children because they could never be breadwinners, and that meant more single moms and fewer father figures in the community.

He learned about his own personal behavior, like where he could smoke his cigarettes and where not.

He learned when to wear his leather bomber jacket and tattered jeans and when to wear his signature neatly pressed slacks and button-down shirt without tie.

He learned to consult Professor McKnight about places where Alinsky's theory didn't match the reality he saw around him.

He learned to consult Professor Wilson about what kind of education the South Side needed to get a foothold in the new economy.

And he became an ace at getting people riled up, just like the Marc Antony funeral speech in *Julius Caesar*.

As Mike Kruglik told *The New Republic*, "He was a natural, the undisputed master of agitation, who could engage a room full of recruiting targets in a rapid-fire Socratic dialogue, nudging them to admit that they were not living up to their own standards. He could be aggressive and confrontational. With probing, sometimes personal questions, he would pinpoint the source of pain in their lives, tearing down their egos just enough before dangling a carrot of hope that they could make things better."

He learned how to face the enemy. He learned that Chicago Housing Authority bureaucrats were crass and crafty and sometimes brutal. He learned that mobilizing ordinary South Siders to confront Chicago bureaucrats meant giving them confidence, telling them who to see and what to say and always being there to back them up – and making sure they got the credit, not him.

And he learned that being black is more about what's inside than out.

Perhaps most important, he learned to be pragmatic. He learned that getting strong-minded leaders to work together required incredible listening skills and superhuman will to keep your mouth shut when antagonistic viewpoints threatened to mire the group in deadlock. He also had the crucial gift of sensing *the group*'s self interest as the individuals squabbled, and then quietly suggesting solutions that made it sound like he agreed with everyone in the room. He wasn't conflict-averse, but his instinct was to find an acceptable compromise, not impose an agenda according to the training manual. The old-timers began to respect this persistent and perceptive young man and to trust him.

He was becoming a politician.

Kellman told the *Chicago Tribune*, "He did not like personal confrontation. He had no trouble challenging power and challenging people on issues. When it came to face-to-face situations, he valued civility a great deal. When it came to negotiating conflict, he was very good at that. He was not one to get drawn into a protracted conflict that involves personalities."

Finally, all this learning paid off. Obama drew firm commitments from a few daring pastors. It took until September of 1986 to get the Developing Communities Project incorporated with Rev. George W. Waddles, Sr., (Zion Hill Missionary Baptist Church) as president, and Rev. Alvin Love (Lilydale First Baptist Church), as treasurer (now president).

But he had done it. When the IRS granted its tax-exempt status the next year, DCP's exempt purpose said: "Community organizing through local church leaders and Developing Communities Project's personnel to improve education, housing, employment and to reduce crime in the southside neighborhoods of Chicago."

Once you organized a group of seduced friends, you needed an action plan to screw the enemy, one that followed Alinsky's Third Rule for Radicals: *Wherever possible go outside of the experience of the enemy. Here you want to cause confusion, fear and retreat.*

How community organizers did that has evolved over time, but a few years before Alinsky died in 1972, a group of his students formed the Midwest Academy and gave *their* community organizing students an agenda sheet that said:

> Being right is not enough.
>
> An organization must also have the power to compel the person who makes the decision to give the group what it wants. In every case there are strong forces on the other side that are trying to make that decision go in the wrong way. Strategy is about getting that power. The key lies in figuring out the cost to the Decision Maker of various ac-

tions that your organization can take in the public arena, so that you can get concessions for not taking them. This is why thinking strategically matters.

The principle is somewhere between a protection racket and blackmail, something Alinsky may have picked up from Al Capone. The difference is, it's not illegal.

With enough money and enough activists behind it, community organizing could undermine America's form of government. Deputizing the Have-Nots to take from the Haves could become the central organizing principle of American life. Think of all the "czars" President Obama has appointed and installed without the scrutiny of Senate confirmation.

That's a matter of real concern, because Alinksy activists and the money behind them will never go away. It's against their rule book.

Alinsky's Tenth Rule for Radicals is: *The major premise for tactics is the development of operations that will maintain a constant pressure upon the opposition. It is this unceasing pressure that results in the reactions from the opposition that are essential for the success of the campaign.*

That's a pretty sophisticated plan.

Unceasingly attack us with things "outside of our experience," so we react with "confusion, fear, and retreat." Then take what's ours and give it to others.

That's what community organizers really do, straight from the inventor.

That's what Obama was taught in those seminars and in three years of street experience.

For all his civility, a socialist instinct gestating within had budded, and it was centered on race: he had learned to be black and seethed to cure the injustices blacks had to suffer.

Power hunger.

As he entered his third year at the Developing Communities Project, Obama was in control of things. His DCP staff had grown from one to thirteen and its revenue from $70,000 to $400,000. He had helped set up a job training program, a college preparatory tutoring program, and a tenants' rights organization. He helped activist Hazel Johnson organize a campaign to remove asbestos from many of the units in Altgeld Gardens. He did consulting and instructing jobs for Greg Galluzo's Gamaliel Foundation – one of those jobs introduced him to ACORN, the controversial Association of Community Organizations for Reform Now.

Chicago ACORN's lead organizer, Madeline Talbott, had watched Obama's talent develop for more than a year, and contracted with Gamaliel to have him give power seminars for her organizers. He had not only become an expert in charting Alinsky's power diagrams and how to research power flows, but also grew into an outstanding instructor.

When Obama later entered politics, ACORN was there to work for him because of what he did with Kellman, Kruglik, and Galluzo: Talbott said, "Barack has proven himself among our members. He is committed to organizing, to building a democracy. Above all else, he is a good listener, and we accept and respect him as a kindred spirit, a fellow organizer."

He was also admired for his skill at fighting the enemy – he never went to the extremes that ACORN did, like getting themselves arrested for storming a Chicago City Council meeting; breaking the law would end his political career before it started. Instead, he meticulously prepared his members for confrontations with officials, charting out who would bring up which points in what order, standing quietly in the back of the room with a clipboard, calling on well-briefed backups if somebody got too nervous to say their piece.

In one such confrontation he had 600 members demanding city action on a water contamination problem – a raw show of power big enough to scare officials so he didn't need to threaten action in the public arena. They could pretty well imagine what would happen if they didn't fix the pipes and toilets and drains. Obama was just that guy in the neatly pressed slacks and button-down shirt smiling in the back of the crowd.

Alsinsky's First Rule of power tactics: *Power is not only what you have but what the enemy thinks you have.*

By early 1988, Obama began to feel a pull. He had spent three years on the streets of Chicago in about the toughest political environment in America. He had a clear view of what was possible.

And what wasn't.

A good organizer, Johnnie Owens, had left the citywide advocacy group Friends of the Parks to join Obama at the Developing Communities Project. They worked well together. Like all organizers, Owens kept a journal so he could file weekly reports of his interactions with the inner-city community. Obama did, too, but he also maintained a second journal, one of "personal recollections and things like that," according to Owens.

For a writer, this world of crumbling tenements is good material. One day Obama showed Kellman and Kruglik two short stories he had written. Both stories were about a minister of a storefront church in the inner city.

According to *GQ*'s Robert Draper, Kellman reads them and thinks, "Hmm. Really strong on character. Still struggling with dialogue."

Kruglik wondered, "Man, all this evocative description of the landscape and deterioration on the South Side in wintertime, the gray sky.... Am I sure Barack actually wrote these?"

These weren't just vivid short stories about pastors and crumbling communities, they were part of a technique Obama had picked up from the writings of Derrick Bell, the first black tenured professor at Harvard Law School. Bell emphasized how traditional legal methods, particularly tightly reasoned courtroom discourse, perpetuated white superiority, and instead advocated using a narrative style, telling stories and anecdotes to examine racial issues within the context of their economic and social and political impacts from a legal standpoint. It suited Obama perfectly.

Kellman and Kruglik didn't realize that their one-time star pupil and now respected colleague was writing up *cases* – the facts of the case, the evidence, the witness testimony, Derrick Bell-style – honing skills for another world.

Obama had been studying Alinsky again, looking for answers, particularly in the changes Alinsky made late in life. He could now see that Alinsky, for all his bluster and rhetoric, was never as big on ideology as he was on methodology. You don't get power by preaching *what* to believe, you get power by teaching people *how* to work out their own destiny – socialism with a new twist. It had to have patience. In his Prologue to *Rules for Radicals*, Alinsky wrote:

> Any revolutionary change must be preceded by
> a passive, affirmative, non-challenging attitude to-

ward change among the mass of our people. They must feel so frustrated, so defeated, so lost, so futureless in the prevailing system that they are willing to let go of the past and change the future.

This acceptance is the reformation essential to any revolution. To bring on this reformation requires that the organizer work inside the system, among not only the middle class but the 40 per cent of American families -- more than seventy million people – whose income range from $5,000 to $10,000 a year.

What kind of leftist would say *that*? Obama saw that Alinsky leaned leftward in general, but had personally detested the Che Guevara wannabes and loathed trainees who carried around Mao's Little Red Book because they were lousy organizers. Marxists were collectivists who didn't give a damn about individual self-interest, and self-interest was the whole reason his tactics worked. Alinsky once told *Playboy* that Marxism was "as germane to our highly technological, computerized society as a stagecoach on a jet runway at Kennedy Airport."

Conservatives who never read the fifty volumes of Marx except for the Communist Manifesto thought Alinsky was a Marxist. He wasn't.

He was a socialist, true enough. But it was his own brand, gleaned from a lifetime's experience.

His early beliefs stemmed from the Social Gospel that flourished when he was young, a movement that applied Christian ethics to social problems, especially poverty, inequality, liquor, crime, racial tensions, slums, bad hygiene, child labor, weak labor unions, poor schools, and the danger of war.

But Alinsky didn't like the Social Gospel's opposition to "rampant individualism," and saw self-interest as the key motivator to social action – and social action was what created power.

Social action could commandeer government and use its police power to take from the Haves and give to the Have Nots.

Alinsky gathered a jigsaw puzzle of socialistic thinking and melded it as best he could into a pragmatic technique for class struggle centered on power.

He died without spelling out his socialism point-by-point, but Professor John L. McKnight, Alinsky friend and Obama mentor, helped two Chicago community groups come close to doing it for him. McKnight was a director of the National Training and Information Center, and its belligerent sister organization, National People's Action, both founded in 1972. Their credo may be closer to a generic "Chicago Socialism," but it's sufficiently like Alinsky's to make it worth quoting:

- Every person has innate dignity, beauty, and worth, and thus is entitled to basic human rights;

- All people, regardless of race, class, gender, sexual orientation and national origin must be ensured a high quality of life;

- Society should be organized on the basis of mutual responsibility, cooperation, and community self-determination achieved through political and economic democracy.

- Take back our power to use the government as our tool to promote the common good, correct the injustices of the past, and redistribute resources equitably and sustainably.

- Democratize the market to put people above profits.

- Enforce fundamental human rights standards that prevent exploitation of people and the environment.

- Take action to ensure racial, gender, economic, and immigrant justice in all social and economic systems.

We may surmise that these champions of the Have-Nots want:

- the government to support them in style ("ensure a high quality of life");

- the government to give money reparations to blacks for slavery and segregation ("correct the injustices of the past");

- the government to own all means of production, control all business and commerce, and confiscate all profits ("democratize the market");

- the government to enforce an all-powerful income-control system for everyone ("redistribute resources equitably and sustainably"). the government to make the writers of these demands the new Haves and make their opponents into the new Have-Nots ("take back our power to use the government as our tool").

If you can visualize an America actually run that way, you can see that it's considerably worse than Marx's dream of a utopian "workers' paradise" and might end up being a step down from Lenin's "dictatorship of the proletariat" and even Stalin's "Great Purge" – what would they do to all the former Haves?

It would be merciless, implacable power unlike anything America has seen.

In 1988, Obama saw Alinsky's whole life's work in that one word: power.

But there was a problem.

By the end of his life, Alinsky came to see something that changed the game: the power in America had trickled down far into the vast and affluent middle-class. Now it was necessary to form power alliances between the Have-Nots and the Have-Some-Want-Mores. He wrote:

> Tactics must begin within the experience of the middle class, accepting their aversion to rudeness, vulgarity, and conflict. Start them easy, don't scare them off. The opposition's reactions will provide the "education" or radicalization of the middle class. It does it every time.

It didn't. Alinsky forgot one thing: the middle class already had a university education (and intact families, paid-up mortgages, creature comforts, and decent careers), unlike the 50-percent school dropout communities he was used to working with.

He forgot his own prime directive: being radicalized wasn't in the self-interest of the middle class. His attempts to make them rude, vulgar and belligerent convinced only a few liberal true believers who enjoyed being bused to the front yards of corporate executive homes, carrying signs and shouting obscenities before being bused back to their BMWs and driving home to their own gated communities.

Alinsky's dilemma: his method didn't work on the middle class.

Could Obama's more civil version of Alinsky work?

Obama made his decision. He'd developed an understudy, as all climbers do: Johnnie Owens would make a good replacement for him as executive director.

That was when he told a few organizer buddies that he needed that Harvard Law School credential to enter the corridors of power – political power.

Owens understood. He told the *Chicago Reader*, "What I liked about Barack immediately is that he brought a certain level of sophistication and intelligence to community work. He had a reasonable, focused approach that I hadn't seen much of. A lot of organizers you meet these days are these self-anointed leaders with this strange, way-out approach and unrealistic, eccentric way of pursuing things from the very beginning. Not Barack. He's not about calling attention to himself. He's concerned with the work."

Getting a Harvard law degree struck Owens as the logical thing for Obama to do.

Obama asked Professor McKnight for a favor, a letter of recommendation, which McKnight generously provided, with the caution, "Don't compromise your principles."

That is, don't forget you're a socialist while you try to get along with everybody in the room.

In May of 1988, Barack Obama quit his job with the Developing Communities Project.

Just before he left, he wrote a "hail and farewell" essay called, *Why Organize? Problems and Promise in the Inner City*, partly to soothe those upset by his departure, partly to soothe himself. Sangamon State University agreed to publish it in the August/ September edition of their periodical, *Illinois Issues.*

It was four pages long, and proved Obama had already mastered the eloquent oration. His parting thoughts:

> Finally, community organizations and organiz-
> ers are hampered by their own dogmas about the
> style and substance of organizing. Most still prac-
> tice what Professor John McKnight of Northwestern
> University calls a "consumer advocacy" approach,
> with a focus on wrestling services and resources
> from the outside powers that be. Few are thinking
> of harnessing the internal productive capacities,

both in terms of money and people, that already exist in communities...

Nowhere is the promise of organizing more apparent than in the traditional black churches. Possessing tremendous financial resources, membership and — most importantly — values and biblical traditions that call for empowerment and liberation, the black church is clearly a slumbering giant in the political and economic landscape of cities like Chicago. A fierce independence among black pastors and a preference for more traditional approaches to social involvement (supporting candidates for office, providing shelters for the homeless) have prevented the black church from bringing its full weight to bear on the political, social and economic arenas of the city...

Through the songs of the church and the talk on the stoops, through the hundreds of individual stories of coming up from the South and finding any job that would pay, of raising families on threadbare budgets, of losing some children to drugs and watching others earn degrees and land jobs their parents could never aspire to — it is through these stories and songs of dashed hopes and powers of endurance, of ugliness and strife, subtlety and laughter, that organizers can shape a sense of community not only for others, but for themselves.

Obama left Chicago.

He took some time off, traveled for three weeks in Europe – where he had never been before – then went on to Africa, to Kenya, where he took five weeks visiting many of his father's relatives for the first time.

When he returned from Kenya in the fall, he was admitted to Harvard Law School.

He needed that Harvard Law School credential to enter the corridors of power – political power.

Now he *wanted* that power.

His power hunger had come from community organizing in

Chicago.

Lizza was right: It's all about power.

The ability to make others do what you want whether they want to or not.

Whack!

Obama Democrats

Washington Post staff writer Joel Garreau once tried to explain why people all over the world want to live in America:

> The traditional deal America has offered immigrants is work, pay taxes, learn English, send your kids to school and stay out of trouble with the law, and we'll pretty much leave you alone.

We'll pretty much leave you alone. The traditional American deal.

Obama Democrats don't get it. They can't leave anybody alone.

Worse, they can't leave our constitutional rights alone.

It's that *power* thing.

A First Amendment example:

In mid-2009, Representative Kevin Brady, Republican of Texas, sat in his office trying to figure out the Obama Democrats' 1,018-page health care reform bill.

Brady had read the whole murky, confusing bill, right down to Division C, Title V, Subtitle D, Section 2531.

He was "granular" (Congress-speak for "knows the details") on the entire bill, including all the geeky lingo: Adverse Selection, Comparative Effectiveness, Cost Shifting, and so on.

But he simply couldn't visualize how the monster mess was supposed to *work.*

That was bad, because Brady was the Ranking House Republican Member of the Joint Economic Committee, created by law in 1946 to review and improve economic policy.

If the health care bill baffled him, it would baffle the public.

Obama Democrats had already rushed the massive bill through votes in two committees with no chance to read it, but it got stuck when fiscally conservative Blue Dog Democrats defied Obama and refused to go along because of its centerpiece – a government-insurance option – which looked disastrous for both the economy and the personal choices of all Americans.

But Democrat House Speaker Nancy Pelosi vowed that the health care bill – which most of its supporters had never read – would pass if she brought it to a vote.

What to do?

Brady recalled that back in 1993, then-First Lady Hillary Clinton's government-run healthcare scheme was depicted on a chart that made its workings visible. So, Rep. Brady instructed his staff to do the same with "Obama's Thousand Pages."

The result, said the Capitol Hill newspaper *Roll Call,* resembled "a board game: a colorful collection of shapes and images with a web of lines connecting them," revealing "a complicated menagerie of government offices and programs" that would be created if the Democrat health care plan became law.

Brady's chart showed *31 new federal agencies, commissions and mandates that come between a patient and doctor* under the Democrat plan.

Now Brady could see the whole enormous, scary jumble. So could everybody else.

He gave the chart to fellow Republicans, who immediately sent copies to the House Mailroom for distribution to all their constituents.

Democrats stopped them cold.

How could they do that?

How could Democrats violate the First Amendment rights of Republicans – *in Congress?*

Here we have to poke into one of those arcane corners of the House that remind us why Otto von Bismarck once said, "Laws are like sausages, it is better not to see them being made."

This congressional sausage is the committee on free mail, usually called the Franking Commission, or, technically, the bipartisan Commission on Congressional Mailing Standards.

It exists because one of the perks of being a member of Congress is that you get to send "franked" — or free — mail, as long as it relates to official business. Lawmakers "frank" newsletters and legislative updates to constituents all the time. Free mail. Very good deal.

The job of the bipartisan, six-member, half-Dem, half GOP, Franking Commission is to make sure that the very good deal is not abused – like sending out re-election campaign propaganda or personally attacking another member. A majority must approve each piece that goes out of the House Mailroom. Mail is very rarely blocked, usually for sneaking in some totally egregious "vote-for-me" or "John Doe is a crook" message.

But the three Democrats on the commission blocked the Republican health care chart.

Because it was electioneering? Or a personal attack?

No. Because it was "inaccurate."

At least that's what they said in an eight-point memo – obviously written by a flock of staff lawyers – claiming that the chart was "misleading" in dozens of places.

The Republican staffers pointed out that their chart reflected the Democrat bill point-by-point. It just made all of the gobbledygook visible – *31 new federal agencies, commissions and mandates,* starkly, horrifyingly, clearly, *visible.*

That was the real problem: anyone could see the bureaucratic morass in the health care bill that would ration care by paperwork delays – you're dead before your surgery is approved. Democrats couldn't allow people to find out. It would infuriate America and kill their bill.

So they censored the chart.

Brady told reporters, "This is the most outrageous example of censorship since I've been to Congress. It's not censorship of Republican members. It's of America."

Republican staffers said this kind of censorship of the minority by the majority is almost unheard of on Capitol Hill, certainly during the years the GOP was in power. Moreover, they said, it was a clear sign that the Republicans were, for the moment, winning a fight once thought unwinnable.

Of course, the forbidden chart instantly appeared on congressional websites, beyond the reach of the House Mailroom. Overnight, it got more downloads than nude celebrities and dating personals combined.

Two days later, Google News posted over 100 stories about the censored chart, most of them with links to a nice, big, readable graphic file showing all the guilty details.

President Obama was not happy.

Within days, the House leadership called a marathon five-hour caucus meeting of all Democratic members in a big room in the Capitol basement for a seminar on what was in the bill, how to understand it, and what to take back to constituents.

No one had ever seen so many congressmen sitting in one place for so long, with staff members from three committees as school teachers going through the bill, section by section, just so Obama Democrats could say they really had read it.

The effect of the chart on the outcome? It's debatable.

But the effect of the Obama Democrat censorship is not.

It got really nasty when congressmen began holding Town Hall health care meetings across the nation and found themselves besieged by angry opponents shouting objections in one district after another.

At first, Obama Democrats claimed the boisterous protests were being orchestrated by the same insurance companies that House Speaker Nancy Pelosi had called "villains." The protesters were "spreading misinformation," she said – the same claim Democrats made about Kevin Brady's "death by delay" chart.

When no Astroturf front groups could be found, and the throngs of protesters kept flooding Town Meetings and shouting down congressmen, the Pelosi gang cranked up their rhetoric to full force.

Pelosi and Majority Leader Steny Hoyer wrote an op-ed in *USA TODAY* where they said that an "ugly campaign is underway not merely to misrepresent the health insurance reform legislation, but to disrupt public meetings and prevent members of Congress and constituents from conducting a civil dialogue."

These are the same liberals who sat quietly smiling when gay rights activists from ActUp! disrupted meeting after uncivil meeting with insults and obscenities, and who thought it was just fine that animal rights activists from PETA protested hearings about eco-terrorism bombings and arsons "to save nature."

Then the hammer came down: "Drowning out opposing views is simply un-American," wrote Pelosi and Hoyer.

Protest by the Left is okay. Protest by the Right is un-American.

Even Obama cringed. He tried to run away from that as fast as his teleprompter legs could carry him. He had Deputy Press Secretary Bill Burton tell reporters, "I think there's actually a pretty long tradition of people shouting at politicians in America. The President thinks that if people want to come and have a spirited debate about health care, a real vigorous conversation about it, that's a part of the American tradition and he encourages that."

The Obama Democrats in Congress didn't budge, but just stopped holding live Town Meetings on health care and doing webcasts on YouTube instead, like Wisconsin Senator Herb Kohl, or telephone call-in sessions, like Florida Representatives Debbie Wasserman Schultz and Ron Klein – or just stopped holding them at all, like Representative Baron P. Hill of Indiana.

And nobody fell for Obama's line, because Bill Burton's next words on behalf of his President were, "Now, if you just want to come to a town hall so that you can disrupt and so that you can scream over another person, he doesn't think that that's productive."

How is that different from what Pelosi said? Perfume in a sewer? Obama was still saying the health care debate would be managed, censored, and protesters silenced. He even put up (and quickly took down) an electronic White House "rat-out-your-neighbor tip box."

Politico reported that after a "furor over how the data would be used, the White House has shut down an electronic tip box - flag@whitehouse.gov - that was set up to receive information on 'fishy' claims about President Barack Obama's health plan." Obama was behaving like Big Brother in George Orwell's *1984*.

The Obama Democrats had lost control of the national debate.

But what they were really worried about was more than just health care. The CBS Evening News nailed it: "For some, their anger is tightly focused on healthcare reform. But for others, this issue is simply the final straw."

There were experts, said CBS, who believed "a growing anti-government sentiment, fueled by extraordinary events such as the bailouts of the banking and auto industry, is spilling over into the healthcare debate."

The whole Obama Democrat agenda was getting its first harsh test.

It was a test of character, and they failed.

They exposed themselves as enemies of the First Amendment.

Sarcastic headlines like *How A Bill Becomes Law: Chicago Style* proved that the public realized health care reform was about Barack Obama, not about Congress.

Velvet glove, iron fist.

First Amendment?

Whack!

A Second Amendment example:

The Attorney General of the United States is the only cabinet department head who is not given the title *Secretary*. The Attorney General ("AG" for short) is head of the Department of Justice - the chief law enforcement officer of the federal government. America's top cop.

President Obama's AG is Eric H. Holder Jr., the eighty-second United States Attorney General and the first African American to hold the position.

It would have been difficult for Obama to find a top cop more hostile to law-abiding gun owners and Second Amendment rights.

It's not that Holder is unqualified. He's been a judge of the Superior Court of the District of Columbia (appointed by President Ronald Reagan, no less), a United States Attorney (appointed by President Bill Clinton), and Deputy Attorney General of the United States (Clinton again, serving under Attorney General Janet Reno).

It's just that he's a liberal Democrat with the usual mind-numbing gun control mania, doesn't believe that the Second Amendment confers an individual right to keep and bear arms, and wishes that private gun ownership was totally illegal. His high-level experience makes him that much more dangerous to the Second Amendment.

It might make you gag, and it definitely makes gun owners consider him unfit for the job, but Obama picked him and the Democrat Senate confirmed him.

Not that Holder was a surprise pick for Obama, whose own anti-gun record goes back to his entry into elective politics. Gun rights defender David Kopel has documented Obama's acknowledged opposition to concealed carry rights, and his support for a ban on handgun ownership when he was running for the Illinois state senate in 1996.

And Obama, while President-elect, made people seeking jobs in his administration fill out a 63-part, privacy-shredding, questionnaire that pointedly inquired about their exercise of their Second Amendment rights:

> Question #59. *Do you or any members of your immediate family own a gun? If so, provide complete ownership and registration information. Has the registration ever lapsed? Please also describe how and by whom it is used and whether it has been the cause of any personal injuries or property damage.*

Eric Holder loved it because – as far as I'm concerned – he wrote it.

Why do I think that? It's true that Obama didn't have a Chicago / Alinsky link to Holder. They met only after Obama was elected as U.S. Senator from Illinois in November 2004. But that means that during the two years of his Senate career, Obama knew Holder, who was then a corporate litigator and white-collar defense attorney at the powerhouse D.C. law firm of Covington & Burling. When Obama cranked up his presidential campaign, he sought out Holder, realizing that a high-profile Clinton-era lawyer who "knew where all the bones were buried" would be a great asset, especially when dealing with rival Hillary Rodham Clinton.

Obama brought Holder on board as a senior legal advisor, and even made him one of three members of the vice-presidential selection committee. When Obama won the election and became President-elect, it's really unlikely that senior legal advisor Holder *didn't* write Question #59 of the "spill-your-guts-or-else" questionnaire.

When Holder was asked to accept nomination as Obama's Attorney General, he was hesitant, worried it would revive questions about his role in signing off on the controversial last-minute Clinton pardon of fugitive financier Marc Rich.

With Democrats in firm control of the Senate, Obama's team – even though Holder hadn't yet been thoroughly vetted for the job – didn't think that pardoning a felon who had fled the country would matter much to Senate Majority Leader Harry Reid, and it didn't.

The vetting process revealed many things about Holder that delighted Obama Democrats (and horrified defenders of the Second Amendment).

- As Clinton Deputy Attorney General, Holder had advocated:
  - * federal licensing of handgun owners, which would make any subsequent government effort to identify and confiscate all legal handguns in America an easy task;
  - * a three day waiting period on handgun sales, a delay that would endanger victims of domestic violence who had an urgent need for self defense against a vicious partner;
  - * rationing handgun sales to no more than one per month, denying families adequate means of individual self-defense in an emergency;
  - * banning possession of handguns by anyone under the age of 21, eliminating firearms training and the right of self defense to responsible youth.
- Holder had been a consummate anti-gun propagandist with great media contacts and a veritable

encyclopedia of factoids and sound-bites to vilify the Second Amendment, such as the assertion that, "Every day that goes by, about 12 or 13 more children in this country die from gun violence" – not adding that 18-year-old gang members who died in turf battles and drug wars were counted as "children" for the purpose of that statistic.

- In the aftermath of the 9/11 attacks, Holder had turned to the pages of *The Washington Post*, where he played on the public's sudden fear of terrorism to lobby for a bill that would have given the federal government the power to shut down all legitimate, traditional gun shows as a way to supposedly stop terrorists from buying guns.

- He had urged that prospective gun buyers be checked against the secret "watch lists" compiled by various government agencies.

- During the Supreme Court case of *District of Columbia v. Heller* – the landmark case that struck down Washington, D.C.'s long-standing handgun ban and held that the Second Amendment protects an individual right – Holder was one of thirteen former Justice Department officials to sign an *amicus* brief in support of the D.C. government's anti-gun position. Holder – along with Janet Reno and eleven other former officials from the Clinton Department of Justice – supported D.C.'s ban on all handguns (including a ban on the use of any firearm for self-defense in the home), and argued that the Second Amendment is a "collective" right, not an individual one, emphasizing that belief in the collective right had been the consistent policy of the U.S. Department of Justice since the FDR administration.

The Supreme Court handed down its *Heller* ruling on June 26, 2008, while candidate Obama was out giving stump speeches. Realizing *Heller* could make the gun control issue a campaign killer, he immediately put on his politician hat and confused the issue: "I have always believed that the Second Amendment protects the right of individuals, but I also identify with the need for crime-ravaged communities to save their children from the violence that plagues our streets through common-sense, effective safety measures."

Double talk.

"The Second Amendment protects the right of individuals, *but...*"

But...

"*But...*" came through loud and clear. Gun owners heard it with a jolt.

Sure, he'd always believed it was an individual right – and mules can fly, too.

He was just stalling for time to think of a way to trump *Heller*.

Obama should have stopped there, but he went on:

"As President, I will uphold the constitutional rights of law-abiding gun-owners, hunters, and sportsmen. I know that what works in Chicago may not work in Cheyenne."

Dead giveaway.

What Obama thought "worked in Chicago" was a handgun ban imposed by Mayor Richard Daley's Democrat machine. It worked, all right – at making Chicago one of the crime capitals of America, disarming law-abiding citizens so thugs could rob, rape and kill them with impunity, knowing they couldn't defend themselves.

So city-wide handgun bans "worked" in Obama's mind, even though the Supreme Court had just struck down a long-time city-wide handgun ban in Washington, D.C.

Gun owners could hear the wheels whirring between Obama's ears: "Hmmm, well, the District of Columbia is a federal enclave, so the states aren't really affected by Heller."

Whack!

The next big Obama shakeup for gun owners came during the Senate confirmation hearing of Eric Holder to be the United States Attorney General.

The AG is different from everybody else in government. Alone among cabinet officers, attorneys general are partisan appointees expected to rise above partisanship. In order to uphold their oath to protect and preserve the Constitution, they're necessarily torn between loyalty and independence. Even though Holder would be President Obama's highest legal counsel, circumstances could lead him to appoint a special counsel to investigate and prosecute the President.

Attorneys general have all struggled to balance loyalty and independence, but few succeed. Lean too far in favor of the White House and you corrupt the office, too far against the President and you could marginalize yourself and render the office impotent.

Which way would anti-gun Eric Holder go?

When Senate Judiciary Committee Chairman Patrick Leahy, Democrat of Vermont, led off the confirmation hearing's questioning about the Second Amendment, it went like this:

> *Senator Leahy:* As I told you, Mr. Holder, I am a gun owner, as a very large percentage of people in my state of Vermont are. But do you accept and understand that the Second Amendment guarantees an individual right to bear arms?
>
> *Holder:* I understand that the Supreme Court has spoken.

What? "I understand that the Supreme Court has spoken." That didn't answer the question. And you can just hear Holder screaming silently in his mind, "No, I don't believe the Second Amendment guarantees an individual right!" But what he said out loud was this:

> *Holder:* The amicus brief that I signed on to recited the history of the Justice Department's positions that had been taken prior to the *Heller* decision. Also expressed the belief in that amicus brief, that was signed by a number of other Justice Department officials, that it was our view, looking at the Second Amendment and looking at the applicable case law, that the Second Amendment did not confer an individual right. The reality is now that the Supreme Court has spoken. And that is now the law of the land. I respect the Supreme Court's decision. And my actions as attorney general, should I be confirmed, will be guided by that Supreme Court decision.

Would you buy a used car from a shifty guy who talked like that? Senator Tom Coburn (R-OK) wouldn't. He had heard too many clichés from Holder like, "We won't take your guns away from you hunters." Well, the Second Amendment's not about hunting. Self-defense was notably absent in Holder's view of gun rights. Coburn tried to nail Holder to the floor on what gun control measures he would impose on self-defense in America:

> *Senator Coburn:* You've been -- you know, there's a lot of publicity out there in terms of written statements and previous comments about what you believe about the Second Amendment. Tell me where you sit today, and more specifically, with that thought as attorney general of the United States, what you would do with that.

> *Holder:* Well, I think that post-Heller, the options that we have in terms of regulating the possession of firearms has been narrowed. I don't think that it has been eliminated. And I think that reasonable restrictions are still possible.

Whoa! What was that? *"Reasonable restrictions?"* Where is this going?

> *Holder:* But any time that we think about interfering with what the Supreme Court has said is a personal right, that has to be factored in now with the *Heller* decision and the Supreme Court's view of the Second Amendment.

Get that? It's "the *Supreme Court*'s view of the Second Amendment," not Eric Holder's. And it has to be *"factored* in." Holder just can't wrap his mind around the Second Amendment as an individual right.

He went on telling Senator Coburn about the gun control he could still do:

> *Holder:* I don't think that that means that we should turn away from the efforts that we have made to make this nation more safe, to be responsible about guns and who has them, how they are used. I mean, our effort, for instance, to go after felons in possession of weapons, I mean, should be as strong now as it was pre-*Heller*.

> But I think that there is certainly -- we're in a different world. I think we operated for a good many years with the assumption that the Second

Amendment referred to a collective right. We now know that that is not the case.

And so, we are still, I think, going to have to grapple with that and understand what that means. But I think it is a huge factor. It's a major difference.

That's a lot of stumbling around by a nominee for Attorney General. "Understand what that means"? This is a smart man who knows perfectly well what it means. What he's trying to "understand" is how to get around *Heller*, just like Obama.

But he had still said nothing about guns for self-defense. He was still stuck in the old "we won't take guns away from hunters" routine. So Coburn pressed on:

Senator Coburn: Let me ask you specifically. Many of your statements in the past had to do with guns as far as sporting events. Do you believe there's any assurance given by *Heller* that, outside of sporting use, there's a right to own and hold a gun?

Holder: Outside of...

Senator Coburn: Utilization for sport -- for hunting, for skeet shooting, for target practice. Do you believe that there's a right to own a gun for other than hunting or sportsman's purposes?

Holder: I think, post-*Heller*, absolutely. I mean, that's one of the things that we're dealing with in Washington, D.C., now.

Coburn: What kind of common sense gun regulations would you like to see enacted?

Holder: Well, I agree with President-elect Obama. You know, closing the gun show loophole, banning the sale of cop-killer bullets, things of that nature, those are, I think, the things that we need to focus on. Those are things I think have a law enforcement component to them. Those are things that I think are still viable in a post- *Heller* world.

We'll pretty much leave you alone. No, Obama Democrats just don't get it.

The Senate confirmed Holder, and defenders of the Second Amendment gritted their teeth in anticipation of an attack on the Heller decision.

Within weeks of taking office, Holder attacked. He told reporters he planned to push for reinstating the ban on so-called "assault weapons" – a media-invented term with no technical meaning, but including many ordinary hunting rifles – which had expired in 2004.

Holder said that he was simply repeating a position that Obama had taken on numerous occasions during the campaign, but he knew it was at a time when the White House was desperate to win over pro-gun moderate Democrats in Congress.

"It's not what we wanted to talk about," one annoyed White House official told *Newsweek*. He complained that Holder and his staff are not sufficiently attuned to the political needs of the White House.

Now we are faced with exactly the Obama Democrat the Second Amendment does not need. Eric Holder knows he has risen as high as he can. He does not see the president's political fortunes as his primary concern. He gives every indication of hoping to overturn or outwit the Supreme Court's Heller decision, whether by onerous regulation, by aggressive litigation, or by cunning stealth.

His goal? The Second Amendment does NOT guarantee an individual right.

The situation is simple: Eric Holder personally rules the Obama Department of Justice.

Velvet glove? Iron fist?

What do you need those for if you're America's Worst Loose Cannon?

Second Amendment?

Bam!

Liberal v. Liberty

We the People of the United States, in Order to form a more perfect Union, establish Justice, insure domestic Tranquility, provide for the common defense, promote the general Welfare, and secure the Blessings of Liberty to ourselves and our Posterity, do ordain and establish this Constitution for the United States of America.

Preamble, U.S. Constitution, adopted in Philadelphia, 1787

Barack Obama appeared in 2001 on a public radio panel discussion and said of the United States Constitution, "I think it is an imperfect document, and I think it is a document that reflects some deep flaws in American culture."

He added that, "it also reflected the fundamental flaw of this country that continues to this day."

What was he thinking?

In another broadcast of the same series, Obama said, "the Constitution is a charter of negative liberties. Says what the states can't do to you. Says what the federal government can't do to you, but doesn't say what the federal government or state government must do on your behalf."

Government *must* do on your behalf?

Didn't he read that part about providing for military defense, civil peace, and courts?

What was he thinking?

Obama added, "And one of the tragedies of the civil rights movement was, because it became so court-focused, there was a tendency to lose track of the political and community organizing and activities on the ground that are able to put together the actual coalition of powers through which you bring about redistributive change."

Redistributive change?

We know what he was thinking: Alinsky's *Rules for Radicals*, not the U.S. Constitution.

Yet Obama took an oath to "preserve, protect, and defend" that Constitution.

Three times, just to get it word perfect without a teleprompter – not a great omen.

Did he mean it?

Or did he have his fingers crossed, with some "perfected" version without "flaws" in mind when he swore that oath?

Perhaps he was thinking of rewriting it himself, with amendments to guarantee constitutional rights to welfare, health care, Social Security, vacation time, and the redistribution of wealth?

Or something more on the order of Alinsky's revolution, taking from the Haves by direct action, threats, or bribes, and giving it to the Have-Nots without bothering to amend the Constitution?

The evidence is not encouraging.

Obama's political agenda is the most socialistic in American history.

He has become more meddlesome than even the New Deal of President Franklin Delano Roosevelt during the Great Depression – dismantling the U.S. Chamber of Commerce for opposing him by threatening and bribing its members, for example.

Whack!

Is that unconstitutional?

Not in Obama's Constitution.

He has nationalized huge chunks of America's financial sector, put government in effective control of huge chunks of the manufacturing sector, lobbied for completely socialized medicine, recommended that Supreme Court justices decide cases according to emotion, complained that the U.S. Constitution only put limits on what the federal government can do to you, but doesn't say what the government must do on your behalf, installed some thirty or more unelected, unaccountable "czars" who answer to the president but not to Congress, like race-obsessed "Diversity Czar" Mark Lloyd, and "Climate Czar" Carol Browner, a member of the Socialist International, and people like former "Green Jobs Czar" Van Jones, who blamed George W. Bush for the 9/11 terrorist attacks and got tossed when Glenn Beck outed him on Fox TV – among hundreds of like-minded lower-profile federal officials who are more discreet about their far-left beliefs.

Whack!

Is that unconstitutional?

Not in Obama's Constitution.

Unlike previous presidents, Barack Obama has hidden, masked, or flatly lied about his life history, and swept to power on his personal magnetism in a blaze of nearly religious fervor and no information, stoked by big money donors, left-wing pressure groups, and an Internet-savvy election campaign.

Whack!

Is that unconstitutional?

Not in Obama's Constitution.

Many critics accuse Obama of knowingly violating the United States Constitution.

I think it's worse.

I think he actually believes what he's doing is constitutional.

That fly-whacking episode we began with is more than symbolic, it's symptomatic of Obama's total commitment to Alinsky-type social change, of taking earned wealth from the Haves by direct action and giving it to the Have-Nots who didn't work for it but who he thinks are *entitled* to it – and believing that's a *good* thing.

He can't see what's wrong with playing Robin Hood and using productive Americans as cash cows for the benefit of his welfare constituency.

He could turn America into a nation of Have-Nots with no Haves left to take from.

He's just whacking the Haves and brushing them off to the floor.

"Got the sucker."

Whack!

Other critics accuse him of utter ignorance of the United States Constitution.

I think it's worse.

I think he intimately knows the Constitution like a trained legal scholar.

Because he is one.

You don't graduate *magna cum laude* from Harvard Law School unless you are.

That means we're facing a real problem. Those of us who don't agree with Obama's politics tend to dismiss his brains and his will. Nobody with his views could be anything but a stupid jerk. He's not.

Jerk maybe, but *not* stupid.

It could be fatal to underestimate Barack Obama. There is a very smart and very ruthless man beneath his charming let's-all-get-along civility.

If we're to counter Obama's administration and his deep-seated belief in socialistic government, we need to know why he believes in it and why he thinks it's constitutional. We need to find the imperfections and flaws in his beliefs, just as he finds them in others, and work to correct them.

So we're stuck with the job of digging out his real beliefs.

Where did Obama get his beliefs about the Constitution?

He clearly didn't have them when he got his degree from Columbia University.

Or after two more rudderless years in New York City.

In Chicago, he absorbed Alinsky's revolution by community

organizing, but it gave him no knowledge of constitutional law.

That leaves only Harvard Law School.

What did Barack Obama learn there?

And who taught him?

Strangely, we know.

I say "strangely," because the documents of his entire education are sealed and not available to the American public that elected him, which has raised a firestorm of outrage, protest and conspiracy theorizing.

We don't know Obama's SAT (Scholastic Assessment Test) scores, and we don't know his LSAT (Law School Admissions Test) score. We don't have records of any of his grades – or even what courses he took.

That leaves the whole nation in the dark about what the Commander in Chief might really believe but isn't saying.

I say "we know," because Obama gained early fame as the first black president of the prestigious *Harvard Law Review*. Just about everyone at Harvard Law School who even heard of Obama at the time (1988-1991) has talked endlessly to the media about everything from his Afro hair style, frayed jeans and cigarette smoking, to his views on the constitutional basis for redistribution of wealth, and why he didn't engage fully in the debate over affirmative action that scorched both faculty and students during his years there, and even the 17 parking tickets he got trying to find a place to put his beat-up Honda in Harvard Square.

Most importantly, we know who was on the Harvard Law faculty at the time and who his constitutional law professors were: Laurence Tribe, Derrick Bell, and American law Professor Randall Kennedy – leftists all, deeply embedded in the intersection of racial conflict and legal institutions.

What they taught is what he learned.

And that will tell us what President Obama really thinks about the U. S. Constitution – and why.

Most of us won't like what we find.

But first, we have to grapple with the unanswered question, "How did Barack Obama get into Harvard Law School (HLS) in the first place?"

We don't have his records, but we can pretty well figure it out without resorting to conspiracy theories. Just follow the steps.

The admissions procedure itself is not terribly complicated. The HLS brochure says applicants must provide:

- Application form
- Personal statement (2 pages, double-spaced)
- Resume
- 2 Letters of recommendation
- LSAT score(s)
- Transcript(s)

Harvard Law School is notoriously difficult to get into. Annually, more than 7,000 applicants compete for about 550 seats. Applicant LSAT scores generally chart in the 98 to 99 percentile range, and GPAs average between 3.76 and 3.96.

But that's not necessarily how students actually get in.

Harvard Law School's website says:

> Each application is considered in its entirety, including transcripts, extracurricular and community activities, work experience, personal background, letters of recommendation, personal statement, LSAT score(s), and LSAT writing sample. Through individual consideration, the admissions committee seeks not only to identify individual characteristics that are important to academic success in law school, but also other qualities that promote vitality, diversity, and excellence in the student body. The committee uses no computational methods for making decisions and no "cut-offs" below which a candidate will not be considered. Each year we admit applicants who believed they didn't have a chance. You don't have to fit a certain mold to fit in at HLS.

Those last two sentences are our key. Because Obama's educational records are sealed, almost everyone assumes they would reveal him to be a dummy that needs a teleprompter to remember the alphabet. The HLS admissions committee didn't think so.

What did they know that we don't?

Start with transcripts: Obama has said he didn't apply himself when he began his higher education at Occidental College in Los Angeles, "chooming" like in Hawaii, playing pickup basketball and generally goofing off, so his transcript of those first two years probably isn't too good.

But we know that Occidental didn't flunk him out in those two years, and that he successfully transferred to Columbia University in New York City, which is an Ivy League school that's hard to get into, so it couldn't have been too bad, either.

He evidently changed when Columbia accepted him. In 2005, he told *Columbia College Today*, "When I transferred, I decided to buckle down and get serious. I spent a lot of time in the library. I didn't socialize that much. I was like a monk."

Trying to verify that has been a clue-by-clue detective story.

Obama declined repeated requests from the *New York Times* to release his Columbia transcript or identify even a single fellow student, co-worker, roommate or friend from those years. Most presidential candidates don't block such facts. Most don't have to.

Federal law limits the information that Columbia can release about Obama's time there, but Brian Connolly, a Columbia spokesman, told the New York *Sun* that, "Mr. Obama spent two years at Columbia College and graduated in 1983 with a major in political science. He did not receive honors."

Cum laude honors typically begin at Grade Point Average 3.3 and go up. Obama's Columbia grades were probably higher, but his overall GPA was lowered by his Occidental grades.

Why would I think his Columbia grades were higher?

An important Columbia instructor has come forward with recollections of Obama: Michael L. Baron, who taught a senior seminar on international politics and American policy. Mr. Baron was Obama's thesis adviser for that course. He gave Obama an A in the course and called him an outstanding student, adding," I'd say he was one of the best one or two students in the class. But everyone in the class was oriented to doing something more with their lives."

That endorsement alone wouldn't be convincing, but four years later Baron wrote Obama a letter of recommendation to Harvard Law School. He wouldn't have done that if he didn't believe Obama was worth risking his reputation on.

As we saw in Chapter Three, Northwestern University professor John L. McKnight wrote the other one, so Obama's reference letters undoubtedly satisfied the HLS admissions committee.

Furthermore, one fellow student who took that Columbia seminar with Obama has been identified: Michael J. Wolf, who went on to become president of MTV Networks. He told the *New York Times*: "Obama was very smart. He had a broad sense of international politics and international relations. It was a class with a lot of debate. He was a very, very active participant. I think he was truly distinctive from the other people in that class. He stood out."

Another fellow Columbia student named Michael Ackerman took a political science course with Obama, but not the seminar. He recalls an almost reclusive persona, consistent with Obama's "monk" description. He was "almost chameleon-like, spy-like, slipped in and out. He tried to keep to himself," Ackerman told *The Columbia Spectator* in 2008.

Ackerman added that Obama never stood out to him as a man destined for the White House. "I don't know that I would have put any money on it," he said. That may sound cynical, but Ackerman supported Obama's election.

I think that lays to rest the suspicion that Obama didn't have the IQ to get into Harvard Law School. But, even with good letters of recommendation, it doesn't tell us whether his transcripts were impressive enough to pass muster, and they may well have fallen short.

If so, how did he get in?

Obama could easily have provided Harvard Law School's admissions committee with an outstanding LSAT writing sample with his published "hail and farewell" *Illinois Issues* essay "Why Organize?" that we saw in Chapter Three. It would have been a pretty good "community activities" credential, too.

Then, too, the HLS admissions committee was no doubt impressed by Obama's work experience and personal background because it was so odd. It certainly didn't fit any mold they had ever seen.

His age was no problem: he was 27 years old and five years out of college, which put him in the 5 or 6 percent of admissions who were out of college five years or more. (over 50 percent was one to four years out of college).

His diversity rating must have knocked their socks off: he was the child of a biracial couple, the black one of whom was an African immigrant. With an American mother, that made him eligible for the HLS immigrant-friendly affirmative action program, which boosts an applicant's SAT scores by about 250 points.

So, affirmative action certainly helped Obama get into Harvard Law, but even if that wasn't enough to heal two years of goofing off at Occidental, he had an ace in the hole.

If anything was the tipping point that got Obama into HLS, it was Harvard's legacy policy, a qualification not mentioned in the application instructions.

Legacy programs give preference to the offspring of alumni.

Remember, Obama's father earned a master's degree in economics from Harvard University, so, even though it wasn't the usual undergraduate degree, Obama Junior was technically a "legacy," as such applicants are known.

Does it matter at Harvard?

Oh, yes.

Former Harvard University president Lawrence Summers has stated, "Legacy admissions are integral to the kind of community that any private educational institution is."

Harsh reality: Harvard accepts 40 percent of all legacies that apply, but only 11 percent of all applicants.

A Princeton University study of Ivy League legacy preference admissions shows that legacies get an equivalent of a 160 point boost in their SAT scores

So, even with the affirmative action enhancement, Obama didn't have to be the brightest bulb in the marquee, he just needed to be reasonably shiny, and his legacy status could charge him up enough to get in the door.

But it wouldn't have worked if he was a burnt-out dud.

One admissions officer at Harvard put it this way: "Legacy can cure the sick, but it can't raise the dead."

That's a realistic non-conspiracy explanation of how Obama met his admission requirements to Harvard Law School. If that's how it really happened, and several alumni tell me it probably is, we can see why Obama doesn't want to talk about it.

The committee admitted him in late 1988 and he went to stand in line at the financial aid office, where he met Cassandra Butts, another of the 180 black students at HLS that year (there were 1,601 total students). She now works as deputy counsel in Obama's White House, and has supplied some helpful experiences.

"We were going through the process of filling out a lot of paperwork that would make us significantly in debt to Harvard for years to come," Butts told *PBS*. "We bonded over that experience. I became as close to Barack as anyone in law school."

It had all begun: Obama enrolled in the usual courses in criminal law, civil procedure, property, torts, contracts, and legal research and writing.

He was getting the power.

Whack!

Warping the Constitution

What did Barack Obama learn at Harvard Law School?

Like most of Obama's life, it's weirder than you can imagine.

In the spring of his first year at law school, Obama stopped by the office of Professor Laurence Tribe – recognized as the nation's foremost liberal constitutional law scholar – about becoming a research assistant.

According to the *Harvard Law Bulletin*, Tribe rarely hired first-year students. An L1 – first year law student – doesn't get constitutional law. But Tribe recalls "being struck by Obama's unusual combination of intelligence, curiosity and maturity."

He was so impressed in fact, that he hired Obama on the spot – and wrote his name and phone number on his calendar that day – March 31, 1989 – "for posterity." (And no, he didn't really know that posterity might be interested.)

Laurence Henry Tribe is not easily impressed. He literally wrote the book on constitutional law: he's the author of *American Constitutional Law,* the most frequently cited treatise in that field, has argued before the U.S. Supreme Court 34 times, and is noted for his extensive support of liberal legal causes. Tribe is one of the co-founders of the liberal American Constitution

Society, a law and policy organization formed to counter the conservative and libertarian Federalist Society. At Harvard, he is the Carl M. Loeb University Professor, a position perpetually endowed by the estate of a noted Wall Street mogul. He also serves as a consultant for the global law firm of Akin Gump Strauss Hauer & Feld. Try to top that.

Obama must have impressed Tribe with something more than his weird back-story of being born in Hawaii with an African father, his childhood in Jakarta with an Indonesian stepfather, and being raised by white grandparents who sent him to elite Punahou prep school in Honolulu and helped him through Occidental and Columbia.

Tribe had his own weird back-story: he was born in Shanghai, China, to Jewish immigrants from Europe. His father was Polish and had lived in the United States when very young, long enough to become a naturalized citizen in his early 20's.

Tribe's mother was Russian, and considerably younger than his father.

His parents met and married in her hometown in Soviet Russia in 1940.

They moved with her parents and sisters to Shanghai in 1941 – part of Stalin's massive deportation of ethnic groups including Jews, but luckily avoiding the usual Siberian destination – where Laurance was born in October, just before Pearl Harbor and the Japanese occupation of Shanghai.

The father, who was proud of being an American, irritated the Japanese, who put him in a concentration camp as a noncombatant enemy alien, leaving his infant son trapped in Shanghai's French Quarter with his mother, aunts and grandparents, all stateless persons.

It could have been worse: most Jews in Shanghai were confined to a ghetto that made the French Quarter look like a country club. But young Laurance and extended family remained in the French Quarter during all of World War II, visiting the father only twice.

After Hiroshima and Nagasaki, Tribe's father was released and reunited with his wife and child. As an American citizen, the father obtained transport to San Francisco for himself, his wife and child – but not for the boy's grandparents or aunts, who were left behind, to young Tribe's great sorrow. He promised his extended family that he would grow up to be a doctor and discover how to make them live forever and invent a telephone that could talk from San Francisco to Shanghai, not knowing it was already possible.

The three Tribes left Shanghai in March, 1947 on the steamship SS General Gordon.

Laurance spoke only Russian when he arrived in America a little before turning six – back in Shanghai, he had been a bratty kid who refused to learn English in kindergarten – but once in San Francisco, he refused to speak Russian any more, and quickly learned English. He later went to Abraham Lincoln High School in San Francisco, became a naturalized United States citizen, graduated from Harvard College (1962, mathematics, *summa cum laude*), and earned his J.D. from Harvard Law School in 1966, *magna cum laude,* then worked for a while at the National Academy of Sciences, and finally became an assistant professor at Harvard Law School (1968), receiving tenure in 1972.

That beats Obama for weird by light years.

And it proves anybody can become one of America's preeminent constitutional legal scholars, even someone who is barred by the Constitution from ever becoming president.

I think Professor Tribe hired Obama for exactly the reasons he said: intelligence, curiosity, and maturity, because this icon of left-wing legal theories was preparing to write a fantastic paper that would require a diligent, observant and daring researcher open to serendipity, the happy quality of finding more than you were looking for. Tribe was about to go out on a limb and wanted researchers who would go with him.

The paper would be titled *The Curvature of Constitutional Space: What Lawyers Can Learn From Modern Physics* – which is the zaniest title you'll find anywhere in the pages of the Harvard Law Review.

It would argue that strict constructionist interpretations of the U.S. Constitution were obsolete, being based on the rigid old Newtonian world-view, and needed to be replaced by more modern relativistic notions of curved space and quantum physics concepts of indeterminacy, which would release judges from the original intent of the Founders.

The paper compared Einstein's theory that space is curved by large masses (such as the sun) to Tribe's theory that courts shape the cultural "space" of institutions with "massive" rulings (such as segregation). The point was that major court rulings build social institutions, change perceptions of morality, and unjustly displace some people in the process, just as the sun makes starlight curve around its mass and displaces it from what Newtonian physics expected. Therefore, old wrongs done by courts, government, and the Constitution itself – such as allowing slavery – should be repaired by new broad constructionist interpretations of the U.S. Constitution, including the redistribution of wealth to compensate for old hurts.

The paper also emphasized quantum theory's discovery that the process of studying an object changes its behavior in unpredictable ways and compared that to a court reaching into society with powerful rulings and creating unpredictable consequences – like post-Civil War Jim Crow laws that led to a century of black struggle for civil rights, replete with murders, riots, revolutionary movements, bombings and assassinations. These, Tribe asserted, should be repaired by broad constructionist interpretations of the U.S. Constitution, with reparations for slavery, redistribution of wealth to make up for segregation's poor schools, and special privileges and recognition for their suffering and endurance.

But, as Elisha J. Kobre, another mathematically trained lawyer, noted, Tribe's physics analogy did not particularly add to or enlighten a legal point that others had made before – "that courts should intervene not only when government directly infringes individual rights but also when people are adversely affected by existing social structures that Mr. Tribe asserts have been created or perpetuated by the government."

Kobre added, perhaps ironically, "but it was nice to see a lawyer managing to incorporate ideas of science into legal theory."

Kobre was suggesting that Tribe's "managing to incorporate ideas of science into legal theory" was essentially a clever way to breathe new life into old liberal arguments – and it did: nearly 200 law reviews and periodicals subsequently cited the article, and four courts have cited it.

Obama's later pronouncements on the Constitution are filled with ideas from *The Curvature of Constitutional Space* – to such an extent that the *New York Sun* called him a "space cadet."

What about Obama's role? *The Curvature of Constitutional Space* was "The Paper Chase Meets Star Trek." The premise of mixing Tribe's mathematical expertise with his legal intellect was so edgy – putting old ideas in new clothes – that it could easily become ridiculous, irrelevant, or misleading, as Kobre came close to suggesting. So Tribe was particularly meticulous putting it together, and no doubt demanded the same of his research assistants.

When the article appeared in the November 1989 *Harvard Law Review*, the acknowledgments read:

> I am grateful to Rob Fisher, Michael Dorf, Kenneth Chesebro, Gene Sperling, and Barack Obama for their analytic and research assistance and to Professor Gerald Holton (Harvard Physics Department) for his helpful comments.

That's a major coup. It guaranteed Obama would graduate *magna cum laude* and got him selected as an editor of the prestigious *Harvard Law Review* in his first year at law school, even though his name came last after the second and third year assistants.

Critics trying to debunk Obama's legal achievements wrote belittling remarks about his influence on the article, such as, "maybe he wrote some footnotes for this article – might even have written a little of the text above the line."

That totally misses the point: Obama almost certainly wrote *none* of the *Curvature* paper, but he certainly learned more about the Constitution by helping Tribe research this sprawling 39-page, densely argued treatise, with its references to Supreme Court cases, court influences on society, the role of cultural anthropology, and the findings of physicists Stephen Hawking and Werner Heisenberg, than he would learn in Tribe's actual constitutional law class the next year.

He didn't have to wait for Tribe to put him through the dreaded Socratic method used by Professor Kingsfield, the notorious contracts professor in *The Paper Chase*, to have his "head full of mush" rearranged to "think like a lawyer" – although that would come.

The politically immature Obama got to watch the mind of a brilliant left-wing legal icon at the height of his powers construct a sophisticated constitutional frame of reference that could be applied to government and achieve Alinsky's revolution in the real world by legal means.

Obama *saw at first hand* Tribe turning the negative liberties of the Bill of Rights into positive constitutional obligations for courts to intervene in social issues – and he saw *how* Tribe did the necessary mental gymnastics.

Only Obama could have connected that arcane technical expertise with Alinsky's method of taking from the Haves and giving it to the Have-Nots.

That is a *very* dangerous connection. It could destroy America.

Now let's go back to the opening of this chapter and the 2001 public radio panel discussion, and revisit one of Obama's statements, but in more depth. He said:

> The Supreme Court never ventured into the issues of redistribution of wealth, and of more basic issues such as political and economic justice in society. It didn't break free from the essential constraints that were placed by the Founding Fathers in the Constitution, at least as it's been interpreted, that generally the Constitution is a charter of negative liberties. Says what the states can't do to you. Says what the federal government can't do to you, but doesn't say what the federal government or state government must do on your behalf.

We can trace that entire line of reasoning directly to Professor Laurence Tribe's *The Curvature of Constitutional Space*. The whole paper tells you pretty much what Obama really thinks about the redistribution of wealth and how to do it constitutionally.

That is a legal time-bomb ticking away in the White House.

But, despite its new pizzazz, it's just the old *Gimme-Gimme* State dressed in a spacesuit.

Before we get to Harvard's real thorn in the side of the Constitution, we need a brief look at one black instructor who touched Obama where he lived: American law professor Randall Kennedy.

He came from an educated family in South Carolina - his father often spoke of watching Thurgood Marshall argue *Rice vs. Elmore*, the case that invalidated the rule permitting only whites to vote in South Carolina's Democratic primary. His family fled the abuses of Jim Crow laws and moved to Washington, D.C.

Kennedy got his law degree from Yale (1982) after earning his undergraduate degree from Princeton University (1977) and advanced study as a Rhodes Scholar at the University of Oxford in England (1977-1979).

What got to Obama about Kennedy was the courses he taught at Harvard on race relations law and freedom of expression, especially one that later resulted in the book *Interracial Intimacies: Sex, Marriage, Identity and Adoption.*

If any one person confirmed and validated Obama's blackness, it was Randall Kennedy. And he also confirmed and validated Obama's growing awareness that his bi-racial back-story was a salable commodity that eventually produced his memoir, *Dreams from my Father.*

Kennedy was also outspoken and fearless: he titled one of his books, N*igger: The Strange Career of a Troublesome Word*, which outraged everybody. But Kennedy defended it with restraint and dignity rather than abrasive retorts – something not lost on the civility-conscious Obama.

Kennedy was not strictly a professor of *constitutional* law, but Obama found his legal teachings important enough to include a Kennedy article in the reading list of one of his own courses when he himself taught law at the University of Chicago.

Randall Kennedy was the most forceful but honorable and nuanced professor to bolster the most dangerous element of Obama's election-winning appeal – his unflappable "no drama Obama" resolution and hidden ruthlessness in the face of opposition.

Power, he was learning *real* power.

Whack!

7

Contradicting the Constitution

What are we to make of Obama's statement that the Constitution is "an imperfect document?"

That brings us to another of Obama's constitutional law professors, more important than Laurance Tribe: the prickly, defiant Derrick Albert Bell, Jr, the first black tenured professor in Harvard Law School's history.

He holds a decidedly critical view of the U.S. Constitution that has seeped into Obama's thinking.

In his article, *The Constitutional Contradiction*, Bell argued that the Framers chose the rewards of property (slaves) over equality and justice, and America was off-track from the beginning.

Bell is the reason Obama said the Constitution is "a document that reflects some deep flaws in American culture." The flaws were slavery – plus a number of more complicated things that he got from Bell.

Bell believes that the pursuit of racial equality is futile in a societal structure in which African Americans are permanently on the bottom.

Today, Bell argues that advocates should adopt a strategy that acknowledges the permanence of racism but agitates for equity. That's a recipe for permanent black rage, and would justify a black president to rule by agitation – especially one expert in Chicago-style Alinsky agitation.

Harvard and Bell didn't hit it off well.

Shortly after his tenure in 1971, a white university vice-president tried to purchase a house that Bell had been offered through a school program. Bell saw this as a blatant case of racial discrimination and mobilized his supporters, which angered his detractors, who accused him of being too quick with his allegations of bigotry.

It was the beginning of a wandering crusade against built-in white supremacy.

Bell left Harvard in 1980 to become the dean of the University of Oregon Law School, the first African American to ever head a non-black law school. He resigned several years later over a dispute about faculty diversity. Bell then taught at Stanford University for a year.

Obama studied constitutional law with him only because Bell returned to Harvard in 1986 – and promptly staged a five-day sit-in in his office to protest the school's refusal to grant tenure to two black law professors.

This incident is vastly more important to Obama's career than it may seem at first – he wasn't even at Harvard yet when Bell started this war.

Harvard Law School's administrators claimed they denied tenure for substandard scholarship and teaching.

Characteristically, Bell claimed it was an unambiguous attack on racial ideology: both of the rejected professors were advocates of a new legal philosophy called Critical Race Theory, which asserted that:

- preserving the interests of power, rather than the demands of principle and precedent, is the guiding force behind legal judgments, which require tightly reasoned discursive argument as the only legal standard, shutting out the disadvantaged, and;

- narrative – story-telling with a racial point – was a legitimate substitute in legal proceedings.

Bell was a co-founder of Critical Race Theory.

The legal community found it outrageous. Judge Richard Posner of the United States Court of Appeals for the Seventh Circuit in Chicago labeled critical race theorists the "lunatic core" of "radical legal egalitarianism." He wrote in *Critical Race Theory: An Overview:*

> What is most arresting about critical race theory is that...it turns its back on the Western tradition of rational inquiry, forswearing analysis for narrative. Rather than marshal logical arguments and empirical data, critical race theorists tell stories – fictional, science-fictional, quasi-fictional, autobiographical, anecdotal – designed to expose the pervasive and debilitating racism of America today. By repudiating reasoned argumentation, the storytellers reinforce stereotypes about the intellectual capacities of nonwhites.

Judge Posner wasn't kidding about science-fictional stories in *Critical Race Theory*. Bell wrote a short story called *The Space Traders*, a tale of aliens "in mammoth vessels" who came to the United States from another star system in order to trade priceless goods that would solve America's problems, and told the President, the Cabinet, and Congress that they would accept only one thing in exchange, which a convincing majority of citizens had to approve. As Bell wrote:

> Those mammoth vessels carried within their holds treasure of which the United States was in most desperate need: gold, to bail out the almost bankrupt federal, state, and local governments; special chemicals capable of unpolluting the environment, which was becoming daily more toxic, and restoring it to the pristine state it had been before Western explorers set foot on it; and a totally safe nuclear engine and fuel, to relieve the nation's all-but-depleted supply of fossil fuel. In return, the visitors wanted only one thing – and that

was to take back to their home star all the African Americans who lived in the United States.

Since it's a Derrick Bell story, you already know the ending: "Heads bowed, arms now linked by slender chains, black people left the New World as their forebears had arrived."

Bell thereafter behaved as if his story were fact, not fiction. He became the perfect exemplar of a famous quote by America's foremost black public intellectual, Princeton's Professor Cornel West: "The accumulated effect of the black wounds and scars suffered in a white-dominated society is a deep-seated anger, a boiling sense of rage, and a passionate pessimism regarding America's will to justice."

Bell never asked whether America's blacks, offered the same deal, would gladly give all the whites in chains to the space traders.

Clearly, Critical Race Theory was irreconcilable with American jurisprudence, and HLS wasn't about to give tenure to its advocates. Today, you can find hardly a trace of Critical Race Theory in the legal literature, so Bell's battle with Harvard fizzled out – but his ideas did not.

Most importantly for us, Critical Race Theory has a background that casts light on Barack Obama's later constitutional views.

Derrick Bell and his co-founders didn't just create Critical Race Theory out of thin air: it was a racial version of the 1970s' Critical Legal Studies, a theory that legal decisions are a form of political decision, and that both legal and political acts are based around the construction and maintenance of a form of "social space" – you can see how that influenced Tribe's weird *Constitutional Space* thinking.

It gets weirder. Critical Legal Studies itself can be traced back to what is informally known as "the Frankfurt School," which was a gathering of dissident Marxists in the 1920s at the University of Frankfurt, Germany – dissidents who didn't like capitalism, but didn't like Marx much either.

These scholars developed a critical theory to cope with Marx's total screw-up in predicting that the communist revolution would begin in a highly industrialized society where capitalism had grown decadent and ripe for a revolution that could expropriate great wealth – Western Europe, Germany first – which it didn't.

In fact, during World War I, highly industrialized Germany packed up fugitive communist Vladimir Lenin "in a sealed train" and sent him off to poorly-industrialized, impoverished Russia, hoping he would stir up trouble there. That backfired later.

The Frankfurt School later saw the rise of Nazism in such an economically and technologically advanced nation as Germany as proof that Marx's theory of how societies are supposed to develop ("historical materialism") was dead wrong.

So they became sociologists who gave up the idea of a working-class revolution and set themselves the task of choosing what parts of Marx's thought might serve to clarify contemporary social conditions which Marx himself had never seen.

Adolph Hitler's rise to power in 1933 prompted the Frankfurt School to move to the United States. In 1934, they affiliated with – get this – Columbia University in New York City. Some Frankfurt scholars made names for themselves in American academic circles, including Erich Fromm, Herbert Marcuse, Walter Benjamin and Jurgen Habermas.

Critical theory, as taught in today's sociology and philosophy college classes, is shorthand for *critical theory of society.*

And that's the paper trail behind Derrick Bell's *Critical Race Theory.*

But there's an oral tradition that influenced Obama in Critical Race Theory, and left no paper trail behind it, a tradition from Africa.

Remember, Bell is the descendant of slaves from Africa, where the role of written language was originally played by songs, dances, stories, and histories spoken by reciters who transmitted the tribe's knowledge from one generation to the next – think Alex Haley's *Roots.*

While Bell was a young attorney for NAACP working to desegregate Mississippi schools, Léopold Senghor, first president of Senegal, wrote his memoir about the early black anti-colonial radicals in France, Aimé Césaire, Léon Damas, and himself, who protested against the West's values that disparaged the values of Africa:

> We threw ourselves like an unleashed sword into
> an assault on European values that we summed
> up by the trilogy: discursive reason, technology,
> the market economy, i.e. Capitalism.

Senghor explained himself: "Discursive reason by itself could not comprehend the world in order to transform it; that it was necessary to add intuitive reason, which penetrated facts and things beyond the surfaces."

The core of it was Senghor's famous, "Emotion is black as much as reason is Greek."

He was saying that Enlightenment reason and Aristotelian logic, both legacies of Ancient Greece, stripped away proper respect for emotion from Europeans.

For Senghor, the African is characterized by the emotional faculty, devalued in Western eyes, but for him another way of knowing the essence of things. He described the nature of being a black man thus:

> Water moves him, not because it washes, but be-
> cause it purifies; fire not because of its heat or
> color, but because of its destructive power. The
> bushes, which dry up and become green again, are
> symbols of life and death. This is because the exte-
> rior aspect of objects, in order to be grasped in its
> particular singularity (or peculiarity) is but as sign
> or symbol of the essence of the object.

Without intuition, you can't know the world properly.

French philosopher Jean-Paul Sartre said that Africans see through the barrier of superficial logical reasoning, toward the realm of the instincts and the unconscious, of presence and belonging – of "being-in-the-world".

A little hifalutin, but to the point.

It was the African way, something Derrick Bell was trying to get at generations away from Africa, and something that gripped the young Obama searching for his blackness.

Intuition.

Emotions.

How do you put that into the law?

And what happens if you don't?

"We need somebody who's got the heart, the empathy, to recognize what it's like to be a young teenage mom. The empathy to understand what it's like to be poor, or African-American, or gay, or disabled, or old."

The African way.

Irreconcilable with the Western way.

Sonia Sotomayor, the wise Latina, disavowed the African way.

We can see Derrick Bell's "lunatic core of radical legal egalitarianism" behind that part of President Barack Obama.

And we can see why Derrick Bell made narrative the core of Critical Race Theory.

But let's not dismiss it completely, for a danger still hides there: even the U.S. Supreme Court has had to acknowledge intuition and emotion in American jurisprudence, most notably in Justice Potter Stewart's remarkable statement in a 1964 decision over possible obscenity in the movie, *The Lover*.

I shall not today attempt further to define the kinds of material I understand to be embraced within that shorthand description ["hard-core pornography"]; and perhaps I could never succeed in intelligibly doing so. But I know it when I see it, and the motion picture involved in this case is not that.

"I know it when I see it" became the most famous phrase in the entire history of the U.S. Supreme Court.

The African way.

And Potter Stewart had no known African relatives.

Senghor's colleague Aimé Césaire said it another way: "no race has a monopoly on beauty, on intelligence, on strength."

But that's just another way to say that the African way and the Western way are irreconcilable, with very few points of contact, the insight that led Bell to believe in the permanence of racism.

One of the Founders wrote the same thing, which was common belief at the time.

Thomas Jefferson wrote of slaves in his *Autobiography,*

> "Nothing is more certainly written in the book
> of fate than that these people are to be free. Nor
> is it less certain that the two races, equally free,
> cannot live in the same government. Nature, habit,
> opinion has drawn indelible lines of distinction be-
> tween them."

When Obama arrived in 1988, Professor Bell had stirred up
a different battle on the Harvard campus – he demanded that
HLS appoint a black woman, visiting Professor Regina Austin,
to the law faculty. At the time, of the law school's 60 tenured
professors, only three were black and five were women. The
school had never had a black woman on the tenured staff.

Bell's demand produced the usual vigils, protests, and
turbulent factions that shook law school politics.

Obama was too busy researching for Professor Tribe during
his first year, but he got sucked into Bell's fray at the worst
possible time in his second year: February, 1990 – just after he
became the first black to be elected president in the 102-year
history of the prestigious student-run *Harvard Law Review,* the
highest honor a student can attain at Harvard Law School, and
the busiest.

Obama often had to make the choice between attending class
and editing law review articles – and skipped a lot of classes. His
friend Cassandra Butts was an organizer for the Bell protests
and made it clear to Obama she expected him to give speeches
at campus rallies. He did, at least twice, even though he knew
little about Bell's constitutional philosophy or Critical Race
Theory at the time.

In his boldest moment, Obama inanely compared Bell to
Rosa Parks – the poor seamstress "mother of the modern-day
civil rights movement" who bravely refused to surrender her
seat on a Montgomery, Alabama bus to a white person and
got arrested for it, but she certainly wasn't a high and mighty
tenured legal scholar like Bell, trying to break a glass ceiling for
a black law professor with a $100,000 education behind her.
The comparison drew snickers from his friends and harrumphs
from his opponents.

Obama later took Derrick Bell's course, learning his entire philosophy, which has remained with him in deeply important ways.

We're certain of that because we have the syllabus of the spring 1994 seminar Obama taught on "Current Issues in Racism and the Law" at the University of Chicago, including a "reading packet" (the *New York Times* posted it online in 2008).

Professor Alfred Brophy of the University of North Carolina Law School thought that Obama's course was infused with Bell: "A lot of the structure seems to have come from Derrick Bell's *Race, Racism, and American Law*."

Obama's reading list was full of requirements like "Dred Scott v. Sanford (or Bell summary)," and "Slaughter-House Cases (or Bell summary)," and "Plessy v. Ferguson (or Bell summary)," and so forth.

Perhaps the most telling thing about that seminar is what he expects of his students: it's what he had learned to expect of himself. He wrote in the syllabus:

> I'll be looking for: a) a focused, tightly-crafted argument, and analytic rigor in working through the legal or policy problems raised by your topic; 2) a thorough examination of the diversity of opinion that exists on the issue or theme; 3) a willingness, after having looked at the various facets of the topic, to take a stand and offer concrete proposals or approaches to the problem.

Let's go back one more to the 2001 public radio panel discussion, and revisit Obama's first statement, but in more depth. He said of the U.S. Constitution:

> I think it is a remarkable political document. But I think it is an imperfect document, and I think it is a document that reflects some deep flaws in American culture, the Colonial culture nascent at that time.

African-Americans were not – first of all they weren't African-Americans – the Africans at the time were not considered as part of the polity that was of concern to the Framers. I think that it was a "nagging problem" in the same way that these days we might think of environmental issues, or some other problem where you have to balance cost-benefits, as opposed to seeing it as a moral problem involving persons of moral worth.

And in that sense, I think we can say that the Constitution reflected an enormous blind spot in this culture that carries on until this day, and that the Framers had that same blind spot. I don't think the two views are contradictory, to say that it was a remarkable political document that paved the way for where we are now, and to say that it also reflected the fundamental flaw of this country that continues to this day.

That's Obama's Constitution – on the one hand remarkable, on the other hand flawed.

Cover all the bases, then take a stand.

But where?

Someplace where everybody in the room thinks you agree with them?

Do not underestimate Barack Obama.

He has internalized Cornel West's "boiling sense of rage, and a passionate pessimism regarding America's will to justice," he has absorbed the "lunatic core of radical legal egalitarianism," and he has mastered the power of discursive reason and hiding the truth.

He is now positioned to crush anything he sees as a "fundamental flaw" of this country.

But he is not positioned to "secure the Blessings of Liberty to ourselves and our Posterity."

Under Obama, Liberal and Liberty have become opposites.

Whack!

8

Fairness for Failures

Congress shall make no law respecting an establishment of religion, or prohibiting the free exercise thereof; or abridging the freedom of speech, or of the press; or the right of the people peaceably to assemble, and to petition the Government for a redress of grievances.

First Amendment, U.S. Constitution

In the Obama Era, keeping the freedom of speech and freedom of the press is not just a fight – like banning Congressman Kevin Brady's health care chart from the House mailroom – it's a full-fledged war against American citizens.

It's Obama's *war against talk shows.*

Less than a month after Obama took office as President of the United States, Obama Democrats in Congress began wrangling for control of the radio airwaves by pushing for a law reviving the Fairness Doctrine, an abolished Federal Communications Commission policy that once required broadcast stations to provide opposing views on controversial issues of public importance.

The Fairness Doctrine was a self-made policy, not a law, promulgated by the FCC in 1949 because of concerns about too many applicants for too few frequencies – the FCC didn't want the lucky ones to shut out the views of the losers. It imposed a two-pronged obligation requiring broadcasters to, first, air coverage of "controversial issues of public importance" in the station's community; and, second, afford a reasonable opportunity for the presentation of contrasting viewpoints on such issues.

The FCC abolished the doctrine in August 1987 by a 4-0 vote, after a liberal group lost a lawsuit trying to make the agency enforce it (the Syracuse Peace Council decision). The FCC not only had the right to stop using it, they also suggested that the doctrine be deemed unconstitutional, stating that:

> The intrusion by government into the content of programming occasioned by the enforcement of [the Fairness Doctrine] restricts the journalistic freedom of broadcasters ... [and] actually inhibits the presentation of controversial issues of public importance to the detriment of the public and the degradation of the editorial prerogative of broadcast journalists.

The U.S. Supreme Court had ruled the Fairness Doctrine to be constitutional in a 1969 case (Red Lion Broadcasting Co. v. FCC) but warned that if the doctrine ever restrained speech, then its constitutionality should be reconsidered.

But Democrats were furious when the FCC abandoned the doctrine in 1987.

You have to understand that the FCC abolished the doctrine during the second term of President Ronald Reagan, at a time before the prominence of conservative talk radio and during the preeminence of the Big Three television networks and PBS in political discourse. The White House staff warned Reagan that repealing the policy would be political suicide:

> The only thing that really protects you from the savageness of the three networks is the Fairness Doctrine, and [FCC Chairman Mark] Fowler is proposing to repeal it!

Reagan not only approved of Fowler's move, but when the Democrat majority in Congress immediately passed a bill to make the Fairness Doctrine a law (and not just a self-made FCC policy), Reagan vetoed it and there were not enough votes to override his veto.

So why the Obama-era push to reinstate it by law?

Only one reason: liberal Democrats were insanely jealous of the huge popularity of conservative talk show hosts Rush Limbaugh, Laura Ingraham, Sean Hannity, Star Parker, and Glenn Beck, among others.

Liberals had been driven to fits of despair when the much-touted left-wing alternative, Air America Radio – launched in March, 2004 with buckets of liberal fat-cat seed-money – failed to gain enough audience to survive its first two years, even with *Saturday Night Live* comedian Al Franken as star host (he's now Minnesota's junior U.S. senator). Mounting debts forced Air America Radio to file for Chapter 11 bankruptcy in October, 2006. (It was picked up by two New York real estate investors in 2007 for $4.25 million and limps along now as Air America Media.)

The Democrats' message?

If the free market wouldn't give liberals success on the talk show airwaves, Obama Democrats would have to do it by government regulation.

Senator Debbie Stabenow (D-Michigan) was congressional point-woman on restoring the Fairness Doctrine by law, despite Obama's campaign statement that he didn't favor its return.

In early February, 2009, she was talking to liberal radio host Bill Press about the recent failure of the "progressive" station Obama 1260. The two whined about conservative gloating and the conversation turned to the question of "whether there needs to be a counterbalance to dominant right-wing talk on the radio dial." *Politico* posted the exchange:

> *Bill Press*: Yeah, I mean, look: They have a right to say that. They've got a right to express that. But, they should not be the only voices heard. So, is it time to bring back the Fairness Doctrine?
>
> *Senator Stabenow:* I think it's absolutely time to pass a standard. Now, whether it's called the Fairness Standard, whether it's called something else — I absolutely think it's time to be bringing accountability to the airwaves. I mean, our new president has talked rightly about accountability and transparency. You know, that we all have to step up and be responsible. And, I think in this

case, there needs to be some accountability and standards put in place.

Press: Can we count on you to push for some hearings in the United States Senate this year, to bring these owners in and hold them accountable?

Stabenow: I have already had some discussions with colleagues and, you know, I feel like that's gonna happen. Yep.

Critics called her plan the *Hush Rush Doctrine.*

Oklahoma Republican Senator James Inhofe bluntly accused Democrats of wanting to diminish the influence of Limbaugh and other conservative talk show hosts.

Senator Tom Harkin (D-Iowa), insisted that the Fairness Doctrine is needed not to remove any conservative voices, but to ensure that there are a few liberal shows on the air.

Inhofe was not impressed. "We have a lot of progressive or liberal radio shows but nobody listens to them and every time one tries to get on, they are not successful. The whole idea is that it has to be market driven. I can't think of anything worse than to have government in a position to dictate the content of information going over public radio."

Robert L. Gibbs, President Obama's White House press secretary, told Stabenow, "I pledge to you to study up on the 'Fairness Doctrine' so that, one day, I might give you a more fulsome answer."

("Fulsome?" It doesn't mean "more full," it means "offensively flattering or insincere!" And Gibbs graduated in political science from North Carolina State *cum laude.* Hmm... Maybe it was irony and Gibbs knew what it really meant.)

Whatever, it's reasonable to ask, why Stabenow? What was her stake in the *Hush Rush Doctrine*?

Look no further than who she's sleeping with.

Stabenow's husband, Tom Athans, is widely considered the originator of the "progressive talk radio" format. He was co-founder and CEO of Democracy Radio, which produced left-wing talk radio shows including *The Ed Schultz Show* and *The Stephanie Miller Show*. He departed Democracy Radio to join Air America Radio as Executive Vice President for Programming before it flopped. He's now vice president of the Detroit real estate development firm, Helicon Holdings, LLC.

So, it's no mystery why Stabenow was so interested in the Fairness Doctrine.

What's mysterious is why she wanted to revive the old Fairness Doctrine when a much more powerful weapon against conservative talk shows had been on Obama's agenda for nearly two years.

Go back to November 7, 2007, when Senator Byron Dorgan (D-North Dakota) introduced S.2332, the ominously-named "Media Ownership Act of 2007," with 24 co-sponsors.

Illinois Senator (and announced presidential candidate) Barack Obama was the second co-sponsor on Dorgan's list.

On the surface, the bill looked like it was only meant to promote local programming by radio and television stations. To do that, it would require the Federal Communications Commission to:

- make no new media-ownership rules without a public comment period of at least 60 days;

- separately report the impact of large owners on "the quantity and quality of local news, public affairs, local news media jobs, and local cultural programming."

That doesn't sound too bad: allow for public input on who gets to own media, and report on local conditions. John Eggerton, the well-informed Washington bureau chief for *Broadcasting and Cable* magazine, explained it thus:

> S.2332 would prevent the Federal Communications Commission from voting on any new media-ownership rules until sometime in 2008 and open a separate proceeding on broadcast localism.

Such "localism" didn't seem much of a threat to nationally syndicated shows like Rush Limbaugh's – most cities and towns have at least one home-grown "Rush-Wannabe" talk show host as well as broadcasts of the real thing. Conservative critics suddenly began criticizing "localism" as if it were the new backdoor version of the Fairness Doctrine, which it wasn't.

You found the real disaster when you got down to Section K of S.2332, which required the FCC to:

- establish "an independent panel on increasing the representation of women and minorities in broadcast media ownership;"

- "act on the panel's recommendations before voting on any changes to its broadcast and newspaper ownership rules;" and...

- provide the independent panel with a "full and accurate census" of the race and gender of all individuals holding a controlling interest in every broadcast station licensee in America.

Whoa! *That's* the fiendish threat. Think of the wall chart map of the U.S. you could make out of that census – black woman owner, color me good, white male owner, color me bad – racial and gender profiling of an entire industry by a government agency!

The bill didn't say anything about who gets to be on the panel or how it would operate, not exactly an invitation to open participation and all that Obama transparency nobody can see through.

It looked very much like a Trojan Horse for government-mandated racial and gender quotas in media ownership – break up media ownership by the Haves and redistribute the pieces to the women and minority Have-Nots.

Affirmative action in new clothing.

Class warfare.

Alinsky's revolution.

Okay, but what's that got to do with Obama? He was just an opportunistic co-sponsor trying to look important for his presidential campaign.

Well, not really.

On the same day S.2332 was introduced, Senator Barack Obama and Senator John Kerry (D-Massachusetts) published a co-written online article in *Politico* titled, "Media consolidation silences diverse voices." They wrote:

In recent years, we have witnessed unprecedented consolidation in our traditional media outlets. Large mergers and corporate deals have reduced the number of voices and viewpoints in the media marketplace.

As we look toward the future, we must ensure that all voices in our diverse nation have the opportunity to be heard. One important way to do this is to expand the ownership stake of women-owned, minority-owned and small businesses in our media outlets.

For too long now, the FCC has been putting corporate interests ahead of the people's interests. It's time for that to change.

We need to not only create the opportunity for minority-owned businesses to participate in the market, but also to help those who enter this business succeed. We will keep fighting until we have a free and open media that represents every American in our diverse nation.

So! The "localism" part of the bill hid an anti-corporate subtext: we'll stop the FCC from allowing free ownership of broadcast media by orchestrating public disapproval from our activist constituency to kill licenses, and we're not going to tell you exactly how we intend to "expand the ownership stake" of women and minorities, because you're not going to like it.

Shortly after that article appeared, the FCC voted to allow more broadcaster freedom to own multiple stations, including "cross-ownership" by newspapers and broadcasters. That vote outraged candidate Obama.

The Nation backed Obama's outrage. *The Nation* is America's oldest continuously published weekly magazine (founded 1865) and "the flagship of the left" in its own words. Its editor, publisher and part-owner is Katrina vanden Heuvel (Princeton, 1981 *summa cum laude*, history), who wrote in her mid-December 2007 blog:

Obama has been a stalwart supporter of encouraging diversity in the ownership of broadcast media. An Obama presidency, he has pledged, will promote greater coverage of local issues and better responsiveness by broadcasters to the communities they serve; it would also push for better opportunities for minority, small business and women-owned media firms.

Fortunately the fight is far from over. Obama has co-sponsored a bill in the Senate that would nullify the [FCC ownership freedom] vote. "Congress will not stand by and allow the FCC to move forward with these regulatory changes, " Obama said this afternoon, "and I will urge my colleagues to push forward legislation that ensures any changes will be evaluated and modified in a transparent and inclusive process, and fully takes into account the interests of our women and minority-owned outlets and communities."

Obama was the leading advocate for the bill, not just a co-sponsor.

And he had some kind of plan that "the flagship of the left" seemed to know about.

The bill didn't pass. But let's think about what the Media Ownership bill would have meant if it had: If you restate Obama's slick Washington-speak in gritty Alinsky-speak, you get this:

Under the Media Ownership Act:

OBAMA SLICK: "the FCC has been putting corporate interests ahead of the people's interests. It's time for that to change."

ALINSKY GRIT: we'll disband large chains of radio stations belonging to the Haves by mobilizing mass liberal activist attacks on their licenses;

OBAMA SLICK: "expand the ownership stake of women-owned, minority-owned and small businesses in our media outlets."

ALINSKY GRIT: we'll give the pieces to the Have-Nots, specifically, women and minorities;

OBAMA SLICK: "we must ensure that all voices in our diverse nation have the opportunity to be heard."

ALINSKY GRIT: we'll let the new Have-Not owners pull the plug on syndicated conservative talk show hosts like Limbaugh, Ingraham, and Beck, and replace them with left-wingers like Tavis Smiley, Rachel Maddow, and Lionel.

OBAMA SLICK: "help those who enter this business succeed."

ALINSKY GRIT: we'll make the new Have-Not owners able to afford dumping profitable shows like Limbaugh's because we'll give new subsidies from the federal government to keep them afloat.

OBAMA SLICK: "We will keep fighting."

ALINSKY GRIT: we will never stop until we eradicate public criticism of left-wing Democrat policies.

Unfolding developments would show that's exactly what Obama had in mind.

Enter Julius Genachowski.

While Obama was speechifying in late 2007, Julius Genachowski had just finished chairing the Technology, Media and Telecommunications policy task force for the Obama 2008 Presidential Campaign.

Who is he? An old friend and basketball buddy of Obama: a year younger (born in 1962), he is the son of Eastern European Jewish immigrants who fled the Holocaust. He was raised in Great Neck, on Long Island, and educated in New York City. He earned his undergraduate degree at Columbia University (1985, history, *magna cum laude*), where Obama graduated two years earlier without honors.

Genachowski attended Harvard Law School, and served as notes editor on the *Harvard Law Review* when it was headed by Obama. They graduated *magna cum laude* together in 1991, attended each other's weddings, and have remained close friends.

While Obama returned to Chicago, Genachowski's career took the Washington path. He clerked for a federal judge and two Supreme Court justices, was a staffer on Capitol Hill, and served stints as adviser and general counsel at the Federal Communications Commission.

He left government for the private sector, where he served as a senior executive at IAC/Interactive Corporation (which made him a multi-millionaire), and founded two D.C.-based venture capital firms, Rock Creek Ventures and LaunchBox Digital.

When Genachowski released the results of Obama's Technology, Media and Telecommunications policy task force in late 2007, he blogged, "The response to the plan has been great. One independent comment that stands out: 'If even half of the proposals outlined here were to be implemented, it would fundamentally change the nature of our democracy for the better.' That's why Barack Obama is running for President – fundamentally changing the country and the world for the better."

Genachowski didn't say who he was quoting, but it was Jon Stokes, deputy editor of the *Ars Technica* website. And he didn't quote the rest of Stokes' sentence: "...which is precisely why very few of these proposals have any chance at all of ever being implemented."

The unmentioned headline of Stokes' story was, "The Obama campaign has released an extremely ambitious 'technology and innovation plan' that geeks will either love or hate, depending on how libertarian they are."

That's Obama transparency and honesty for you.

But Genachowski is extremely intelligent and competent, if not too forthcoming. He convinced Obama to run his presidential campaign using innovative technology and the Internet for grassroots engagement and participation.

After Obama won the election, Genachowski co-led the Technology, Innovation, and Government Reform Group for Obama's presidential transition team, working closely with transition leader John Podesta, who was on leave from the Soros-funded Democrat think tank, Center for American Progress – and already knee-deep in Obama's media control plans.

On March 3, 2009, shortly after Senator Stabenow started making noise about reviving the Fairness Doctrine as a law, Genachowski was announced as President Obama's nominee to head the Federal Communications Commission as Chairman.

On June 16 Genachowski sailed through his confirmation hearing in the Senate Commerce Committee, won unanimous confirmation by the whole Senate on the 25th, and took the oath of office June 29 for a 5-year term.

So, Obama had an old friend who had managed his hi-tech online presidential campaign now running the FCC – with intimate knowledge of the campaign's activist Internet responders and email list. If used by a grassroots expert, that information was powerful enough to generate pressure on the agency to do whatever the president wanted.

All Obama needed now was somebody with the intellect, experience, network, and corporate hatred to activate the activists.

Enter Mark Lloyd.

Obama's "Diversity Czar."

Lloyd, a 55-year-old civil-rights attorney, took office on August 4, 2009 in Obama's newly created FCC post of Associate General Counsel / Chief Diversity Officer, reporting directly to FCC General Counsel Austin Schlick, but hired by Chairman Genachowski.

The post of chief diversity officer in the FCC, unlike the same job title in corporations and universities, has no policy-making power and no control over the FCC's budget ($335,794,000 for 2010).

Genachowski called Lloyd's hiring part of an effort to "expand opportunities for women, minorities and small businesses to participate in the communications marketplace."

Obama's Diversity Czar immediately came under fire for his long record of relentless activism against corporate America, his race-intensive outlook (he is a hard-edged African-American descendant of slaves, unlike Obama) and his formidably intelligent attack plan against commercial media.

The *Wall Street Journal* said, "Mr. Lloyd in the past has criticized corporate ownership of media outlets, saying it has led to conservative dominance of talk radio."

The *WSJ* also noted that Lloyd was a senior fellow at John Podesta's Center for American Progress in 2007, and co-authored a report "that proposed ways the FCC could change the balance of conservatives to progressives on talk radio by imposing new rules on the radio industry, such as more frequent license renewals and a national radio-ownership cap."

That Lloyd report, *The Structural Imbalance of Political Talk Radio*, was written in early 2007, *before* the Media Ownership Act was drafted. It was published in April 2007 by John Podesta and another left-wing outfit called Free Press, *before* Podesta became Obama's transition leader. It was well-known by Genakowski and Obama from the beginning, just so we keep all the dots connected.

Investor's Business Daily headlined an editorial, "Diversity Czar Threatens Free Speech," with a subhead reading:

> 1st Amendment: Mark Lloyd, a disciple of Saul Alinsky and fan of Hugo Chavez, wants to destroy talk radio and says free speech is a distraction. The new FCC diversity "czar" says Venezuela is an example we should follow.

IBD editors had discovered Lloyd's provocative 2006 book, *Prologue to a Farce: Communication and Democracy in America,* which took its title from an 1822 quote by James Madison: "A popular Government without popular information or the means of acquiring it, is but a Prologue to a Farce or a Tragedy or perhaps both." The book is a history of how media have gone wrong since Madison's day.

Lloyd used Madison's program of giving newspapers priority delivery in the fledgling United States Post Office to justify his own program of making the government provide citizens with modern communications technology for their political communication, which is something of a stretch.

To be fair to Lloyd, he tells us as much on page 22 of *Prologue to a Farce*, "I am not a historian," he says, and adds that his book is a "*construction* of a political history of communications policy," [his emphasis].

He emphasizes the word *construction* "to acknowledge that I am not providing just the facts," but lenses to view the murky past through "my focus on political equality, my preoccupation with race, my emphasis on the ideas of political leaders."

Lloyd's acknowledged prejudices led him to write scholarly passages loaded with incendiary remarks that give needless offense to American sensibilities, for example:

> (Page 20) As Newton Minow has observed, all too often Americans use the First Amendment to end discussion of communications policy. *It should be clear by now that my focus here is not freedom of speech or the press.* This freedom is all to often an exaggeration. Harold Innis may have been only slightly exaggerating when he wrote, "Freedom of the press...has become the great bulwark of monopolies of the press." *At the very least, blind references to freedom of speech or the press serve as a distraction from the critical examination of other communications policies.* (Emphasis added)

Lloyd's next two paragraphs draw upon quotes from no less than four other scholars, which he salts with derogatory remarks that are easy to lift into newspaper headlines. Here is the second of the two:

> (Page 21) Drawing from Alexander Meiklejohn, Michael Sandel notes that the first purpose of the First Amendment was to provide citizens with the "fullest possible participation in the understanding of the problems" a self-governing citizenry must decide. But now, he notes, while "the courts continue to acknowledge the importance of free speech to the exercise of self-government, courts and constitutional commentators alike increasingly defend free speech in the name of individual self-expression." Thus, the purpose of free speech is warped to protect global corporations and block rules that would promote democratic governance.

This book certainly does not ignore the First Amendment. I only seek to place it in a context with other communications policies.

Most Americans don't think the Bill of Rights is something you can put in a context with other policies, communications or otherwise. The trouble with Lloyd is not that his remarks are taken out of context – they are, extravagantly – it's that putting them back into context makes them worse.

IBD editors did not mischaracterize Lloyd, who did indeed refer extensively in his book to Saul Alinky as a model for activists (pages 249 and 271 through 276), and indeed Lloyd calls for an all-out "confrontational movement" against private media.

As for the Chavez episode, *IBD* editors held up a June 10 video of Lloyd at the 2008 National Conference for Media Reform (put on by Free Press, Podesta's buddies) saying:

> In Venezuela, with Chavez, it's really an incredible revolution - a democratic revolution. To begin to put in place things that are going to have an impact on the people of Venezuela.

> The property owners and the folks who then controlled the media in Venezuela rebelled - worked, frankly, with folks here in the U.S. government - worked to oust him. But he came back with another revolution, and then Chavez began to take very seriously the media in his country.

And we've had complaints about this ever since.

Calling Chavez' revolution "democratic" is strictly Orwellian. Chavez' rigged his election by forcibly moving opponents to "relocation centers" where they couldn't vote, and he used every dirty trick from ballot stuffing to violence to win. His "democracy" was launched by his handpicked "constitutional convention" that shut down Venezuela's elected National Assembly and rewrote its constitution into a 350-section monstrosity. Chavez revoked the license of the nation's oldest television network, RCTV, which criticized him, replacing it with a state-run station that showed cartoons and old movies. He also revoked the licenses of more than 200 opposition radio stations. Lloyd later said he does not support Chavez.

At the 2005 National Conference for Media Reform (an earlier Free Press event) Lloyd spoke about the need to remove white people from powerful positions in the media to give minorities a fairer chance:

> There's nothing more difficult than this because
> we have really truly, good, white people in impor-
> tant positions, and the fact of the matter is that
> there are a limited number of those positions. And
> unless we are conscious of the need to have more
> people of color, gays, other people in those posi-
> tions, we will not change the problem. But we're
> in a position where you have to say who is going
> to step down so someone else can have power.
> There are few things, I think, more frightening in
> the American mind than dark-skinned black men.
> Here I am.

Alinsky couldn't have said it better.

Take power from the Haves, give it to the Have-Nots.

Andrew Breitbart, *Washington Times* commentator,
published the audio of the conference on his Breitbart.com Web
site in September 2009.

With a Diversity Czar as wild-eyed as that, talk radio hosts
feared Lloyd's hiring was a signal the agency was planning to
go after them. Rush Limbaugh, discussing Lloyd with Fox News
host Glenn Beck, said, "The administration is trying to stifle
dissenting voices."

"Mark Lloyd doesn't like corporate ownership of media," said
Seton Motley, communications director of the Media Research
Center, a conservative content analysis organization. "He wants
to use the vast power of the FCC to hammerlock the radio industry."

Bloggers were considerably more colorful. Cao's Blog had
this to say:

> You are about to lose your freedom of speech.

Someone who extols the virtues of the revolution in Venezuela
is most certainly an anti-capitalist and revolutionary....
revolutionary in the fact that it disregards the First Amendment
completely.

"The FCC should be fully funded with regulatory fees from
broadcast, cable, satellite, and telecommunications companies.
The FCC should be staffed at regional offices - at levels sufficient

to monitor and enforce communication regulation." - Mark Lloyd, "Prologue to a Farce" 2006.

Trying to wipe out the opposition - this is about the Obama administration living up to Obama's track record of getting rid of his opponents. He doesn't care for debate; as he said, he just wants those who disagree to 'get out of the way'.

Others wondered if "Diversity Czar" Lloyd would give non-minorities equal treatment. His background as a ferocious, race-obsessed, anti-corporate civil rights lawyer seems to have made race, gender, and victimhood the only things of importance to him: for example, he organized and moderated a 2008 forum as an affiliate professor at Georgetown University's Public Policy Institute on the role of philanthropy in shaping public policy, with the title, "Taking Account of Race: A Philanthropic Imperative," with distinguished scholars emphasizing the need to make foundations specifically racially activist. Diversity was his job title, but would he take his preoccupation with race and hatred of corporations into the FCC?

Ten days after Lloyd took office, Iowa Republican Senator Charles Grassley sent a letter to Genachowski, reminding him:

> On April 22, 2009, before your confirmation by the U.S. Senate for your position as Chairman of the FCC, you came to my office and told me that you did not support an effort to reinstitute the Fairness Doctrine. I took you at your word that, if confirmed, the policies that you promoted at the FCC would not include any policy or regulatory shifts that seek to reintroduce the long abandoned Fairness Doctrine.

But, "given the appointment of Mr. Lloyd," Grassley was concerned that the FCC chairman was "moving away from pledges not to reinstate the Fairness Doctrine." But the senator did not follow that red herring, and went to the heart of the problem:

It would be unfair for me to say that Mr. Lloyd has specifically advocated for a return to the Fairness Doctrine. Instead, he has argued that the Fairness Doctrine is unnecessary if other regulatory reforms to commercial radio are implemented. Specifically, in discussing the Center for American Progress paper "The Structural Imbalance of Political Talk Radio," Mr. Lloyd authored an internet article published on CAP's website entitled, "Forget the Fairness Doctrine." In that piece, Mr. Lloyd stated, "we call for ownership rules that we think will create greater local diversity...we call for more localism by putting teeth into the licensing rules. But we do not call for a return to the Fairness Doctrine."

The single word "Structural" was the key.

• The Fairness Doctrine is about *content* – about *what* the broadcaster says and letting others say differently. It's a weak instrument that leaves the broadcaster's speaker on the air.

• *Structural* change is about context – who owns the broadcast license. It's a strong instrument. Yank the license and the offending speaker goes away. Structural change has nothing to do with the Fairness Doctrine, it simply makes it irrelevant.

Genachowski replied that he did "not support policies intended to reinstate the Fairness Doctrine through a back door or otherwise," and FCC Chief of Staff Edward Lazarus said that Lloyd's work at the FCC "has nothing to do with the Fairness Doctrine or the content of radio or television broadcasting."

Neither said anything about structural change.

Seton Motley of the Media Research Center caught it on the NewsBusters website:

> [Lloyd's "Structural Imbalance of Political Talk Radio"] recommendations get perilously close to the use of "localism" to silence conservative (and Christian) radio stations, about which we have been warning for quite some time.

In a follow-up essay to the CAP report entitled "Forget the Fairness Doctrine," Lloyd specifically instructs liberal activists to do the latter – use the "localism" requirement to harass conservative stations by filing complaints with the FCC. The FCC would then assess these stations fines, with the money going to (very liberal) public broadcasting.

Or worse – the FCC would rescind these stations' broadcast licenses. In other words, shut them up by shutting them down. Thus, as Lloyd says, no need for the mis-named "Fairness" Doctrine.

In mid-September, all five commissioners of the FCC were called to testify before the House Energy and Commerce Committee by Representative Rick Boucher (D-Virginia), chairman of the Subcommittee on Communications, Technology, and the Internet.

At the hearing on "Oversight of the Federal Communications Commission," FCC Chairman Julius Genchowski and Commissioners Michael Copps, Robert McDowell, Mignon Clyburn and Meredith Baker plowed through many technical issues such as broadband expansion, public safety, and reform at the FCC, but said little about broadcast.

Representative Greg Walden, Oregon Republican, talked to Chairman Genchowski about Mark Lloyd: "There are comments – video comments about Hugo Chavez. I mean, there's some pretty outrageous things being said, having been written in the past. And that troubles me that somebody that's that opinionated, to the extreme element that he is – from my perspective, is not going to bring balance to that diversity position that you've created."

Genachowski said Congressman Walden's worries were misplaced. "Mark Lloyd is not working on these issues. He's not working on Fairness Doctrine issues. He's not working on censorship issues. He's working on opportunity issues, primarily now on broadband adoption, focusing on making sure that broadband is available to all Americans."

In response to pointed probing, Genachowski flatly stated to the subcommittee that "I do not support reinstatement of the Fairness Doctrine," and said he would make Mark Lloyd available for congressional testimony, as he would any other FCC staff member.

Nobody said anything about structural change.

Profile of Mark Lloyd:

- Mark Irving Lloyd was born October, 1954 in Michigan. He married Charlotte Elizabeth Martin in 1980; they divorced December 27, 1993. They have a daughter, Kelly Elizabeth Lloyd, born 1986, a 2008 graduate of Oberlin College in Ohio (double-major in African-American Studies and Studio Art, honors), and was awarded a 2-year fellowship in India, 2009-11);

- Lloyd's education came in two parts: first, an undergraduate degree from the University of Michigan (1978, double-major in political science and journalism).

- In late 1978, he began working for Cosmos Broadcasting Corporation (founded 1939, radio and television stations), then Storer Broadcasting, Inc. (founded 1927, radio, television stations with NBC affiliates, and cable franchises, sold in 1985) and then NBC, where he served as reporter and also conducted public response reports on programming.

- By 1985, Lloyd was producing newscasts at CNN in Washington, D.C. He won an Emmy and a Cine Golden Eagle.

- 1990. After an 18-year journalism career, he entered the Georgetown University Law Center in 1990 at age 36 and received his juris doctor degree in 1993. He was admitted to the District of Columbia Bar April 1, 1994 (membership suspended in 2000 for non-payment of dues).

- 1992 Clinton Transition Team and Clinton White House advising the President and the Office of Domestic Policy on personnel, policy, and organizational issues related to arts and communications.

- Worked 3 years as an attorney at Dow, Lohnes & Albertson (Washington, D.C.)

- General Counsel of the Benton Foundation (Washington, D.C.), a private operating foundation that creates and funds its own projects centered on telecommunications.

- 1997. co-founded the Civil Rights Forum on Communications Policy (Cambridge, Massachusetts), an unincorporated project of the Tides Center, formed after a meeting in November 1996 at the Civil Rights Project, Inc. in Boston. The Forum worked with Tides Center from 1997 to 2003, "to bring civil rights principles and advocacy to the communications policy debate."

• 2002-2004, visiting Martin Luther King scholar at MIT - oversaw the MIT Community Lab (interviewed 70 Cambridge, MA leaders on major issues) and taught communications policy.

• He is an adjunct professor of public policy at the Georgetown University Public Policy Institute

• senior fellow, Center for American Progress, 2005.

• Board member of Center for Strategic Communications, Inc.; Independent Television Service; Internet Education Foundation; Cultural Environmental Movement (Philadelphia); OMB Watch; the Center for Democracy and Technology; and the Leadership Conference on Civil Rights Education Fund.

• He has also served as a consultant to the John D. and Catherine T. MacArthur Foundation, the George Soros Open Society Institute, and the Smithsonian Institution.

• board member of the Leadership Conference on Civil Rights/ Education Fund (2002-2006), and Vice President for Strategic Initiatives (2007-2008) where he oversaw media and telecom initiatives. This group signed a petition to the United Nations in 2000 to overturn the free speech clause of the First Amendment to the U.S. Constitution, as we shall see.

As if to reveal the machinery that could easily bring about structural change, the day before the Thursday hearing – just after anti-Obama protests peaked with a Sunday march on Washington of at least 60,000 angry conservatives, the lowest estimate in the range of 60,000 to 200,000 – a carefully orchestrated coalition of more than 50 non-profit activist groups wrote to the FCC urging the agency to speak out in support of Lloyd.

The Washington Post reported:

> Glenn Beck, the conservative host of Fox News, has headed the attacks on Lloyd, who has called for public broadcasting outlets to receive greater funding from private broadcasters. Beck said that Lloyd's proposals, which were outlined in a 2006 book written before he joined the FCC in July,

would hamper free speech and put "voices like mine" out of business.

The advocacy groups, including the Free Press and the Center for American Progress, struck back today, accusing Beck and other critics of making "false and misleading claims" about Lloyd's work

The timing was perfect and the letter was a classic non-denial denial: it did not address the complaints against Lloyd, but instead pointed to his impressive credential as "a respected historian, an experienced civil rights leader and a dedicated public servant," and called his opponents liars.

It did not deny that Lloyd was devoted to Alinsky's revolution, or his fixation on race-intensive views, or his belief that Hugo Chavez' socialist state of Venezuela was "democratic."

Nobody in the media asked how such a vast and varied co-alition could be put together so fast, or even delved into who they were and how they were connected to Mark Lloyd, because nobody realized that vast and varied coalition could be used as the instrument of destruction of every broadcast license in the nation.

Now we must ask and answer those questions:

• Who were they?

• How were they connected to Mark Lloyd?

Because they are the key to thwarting the destruction of American freedom of speech.

The letter was titled, "Public Interest and Civil Rights Groups Speak Out Against Unfounded Attacks on Mark Lloyd," and released by Free Press on their website at http://www.freepress. net/node/72697. Actually, it only had 49 groups on it, but there were probably many more available.

Free Press is a tax-exempt 501(c)(3) organization with a companion 501(c)(4) lobbying group, Free Press Action Fund, based in Washington with an office in Florence, Massachusetts.

Free Press has received foundation grants totaling over $14 million since 2003, over $3.4 million from PBS icon Bill Moyers' Schumann Center for Media and Democracy and more than $800,000 from George Soros' Open Society Institute alone.

Donors include The Partridge Foundation ($1,500,000), the Rockefeller Brothers Fund ($50,000), and many more wealthy left-wing donors.

The first signature on the letter was Josh Silver, Free Press executive director ($105,132 salary, $14,892 benefits).   Why him?

Easy answer: he was Mark Lloyd's co-author of *The Structural Imbalance of Political Talk Radio* at Podesta's Center for American Progress, so he was protecting both a buddy and his own reputation, aside from defending "the cause."

Then too, Van Jones, formerly Obama's "Green Jobs Czar," sits on the board of directors of Free Press, and he had just be forced to resign by pressure from those same "misleading" conservative commentators pestering Lloyd. They outed Jones as a loud-mouthed lefty activist who once unwisely claimed to be a communist (he wasn't ever a party member), and who signed the "Truther" petition that appeared in the *New York Times* suggesting that the Bush administration knew about and could have prevented the 9/11 attacks on the World Trade Center and the Pentagon. His lame excuses didn't wash and Obama threw him under the bus.

So part of Josh Silver's motivation may have been a get-even for one of his board members' fall from grace. That's just a guess. What do you think?

All Mark Lloyd had to do was get Josh Silver on the phone and say, "Help, please." Lloyd knew there was help available not just because Josh was a friend, but also because Free Press is the largest media reform organization in the United States, with nearly half-a-million activists. They could pull off the perfect storm of license-yanking protests if called upon. And getting Josh to help line up 50 or more support groups would be a snap.

The second signature on the letter was Wade Henderson, executive director of the Leadership Conference on Civil Rights. Mark Lloyd worked at their Education Fund as vice president for strategic initiatives just before coming to the FCC.

Since the Leadership Conference is a broad-based coalition, Henderson could just pick up the phone and get help. He instantly got nine of his member groups to sign on, no problem

– and three of them were affiliates of one Conference member, the Communication Workers of America.

It was the same members that had joined Henderson in 2000 in signing A Call to Action to the United Nations, a formal request by thirty-eight civil rights groups to punish the United States for human rights violations.

Henderson was one of the leaders of the effort, and told reporters the groups went to the UN because blacks and other minorities were "frustrated by the lack of response at the state or federal level to endemic racial discrimination," and wanted UN help in "holding the United States accountable for the intractable and persistent problems of discrimination faced by men and women in the hands of the criminal justice system."

Specifically, Henderson's group and all the rest wanted the UN's Committee on the Elimination of Racial Discrimination to make the U.S. Senate obey two contentious sections of the International Convention on the Elimination of Racial Discrimination (ICERD):

- One, to make a crime of "disseminating ideas based on racial superiority or hatred," and to outlaw groups that "promote and incite racial discrimination," and;

- Two, to "adopt immediate and effective measures" to combat prejudices "in education, culture and information."

The U.S. Senate ratified ICERD in 1994, but even the Democrat-controlled Senate during the Clinton administration gagged on that infusion of intrusion, and made their ratification "subject to the following reservations":

> 1. That the Constitution and laws of the United States contain extensive protections of individual freedom of speech, expression and association. Accordingly, the United States does not accept any obligation under this Convention to restrict those rights, through the adoption of legislation or any other measures, to the extent that they are pro- tected by the Constitution and laws of the United States.

2. That the Constitution and laws of the United States establish extensive protections against discrimination, reaching significant areas of non-governmental activity. Individual privacy and freedom from governmental interference in private conduct, however, are also recognized as among the fundamental values which shape our free and democratic society. To the extent that the Convention calls for a broader regulation of private conduct, the United States does not accept any obligation under this Convention to enact legislation or take other measures, to the extent that they are protected by the Constitution and laws of the United States.

Wade Henderson and his Leadership Conference on Civil Rights wanted those reservations removed.

That's what Wade Henderson and his Leadership Conference on Civil Rights and all their fellow signatories think of the First Amendment's freedom of speech clause.

Defend Mark Lloyd? No question about it.

So now we've got 11 groups signed on and half a million left-wing activists riled up.

The third signature on the letter was Winnie Stachelberg, vice president for external affairs of John Podesta's Center for American Progress.

The Center for American Progress was created by a secret "brain trust" appointed by Terry McAuliffe, chairman of the Democratic National Committee to head off the 2004 re-election of George W. Bush. It included former Clinton White House Chief of Staff John Podesta, former Deputy Chief of Staff Harold Ickes, and four others. They needed a liberal version of the conservative Heritage Foundation to generate progressive ideas with a new think-tank and a new lobbying group to slap down election campaign problems.

It was quietly incorporated as the American Majority Institute in 2002, but launched amid much hoopla a year later as the Center for American Progress. It had been paid for by George Soros, bankers Herb and Marion Sandler, and with the help of Hillary Rodham Clinton, who generously provided access to her fund-raising clout through close friend Ickes (he was the brains behind her successful U.S. Senate campaign).

So, now that Hillary was Obama's Secretary of State and his transition team leader John Podesta was running a $26 million-a-year Democratic front group that had published the Mark Lloyd-Josh Silver talk show report, Stachelberg didn't have to do anything but put her name on the letter to let everybody on the left know that they'd better add their names below hers if they wanted to stay on the good side of a lot of very powerful people.

Getting more than fifty groups to sign the letter defending Mark Lloyd was just a matter of going down three or four key lists.

You want the little independent media activists? Call the Media Action Grassroots Network in California. It's operated in Oakland by the Center for Media Justice. A phone call to their dozen or so members got eight more instant signatures:

- Appalshop (Whitesburg, Kentucky)
- Esperanza Peace and Justice Center (San Antonio, Texas)
- Main Street Project (Minneapolis, Minnesota)
- Media Alliance (San Francisco, California)
- Media Mobilizing Project (Philadelphia, Pennsylvania)
- New Mexico Media Literacy Project (Albuquerque, New Mexico)
- Reclaim the Media (Seattle, Washington)
- Texas Media Empowerment Project (San Antonio, Texas)

You want the hi-falutin thinkers in media activism? Call Andrew Schwartzman, head of the Media Access Project. His new associate director, Matthew Wood, once worked for the law firm, Dow, Lohnes & Albertson – and so did Mark Lloyd. Then, too, one member of their board of directors is Kathleen Wallman, former chief of the FCC Common Carrier Bureau who still has friends there. The Media Access Project folks know lots of people among the media intelligentsia who could lend snob value to the letter.

You want the most ferocious anti-conservative media activists in the country? Call Media Matters Action Network Managing Director Ari Rabin-Havt (#42 on the list, but don't let that fool you), a Democrat operative who has staffed for Senate Majority Leader Harry Reid, Al Gore, and the Democratic National Committee, and also co-founded MoveOn Student Action.

He launched a new Media Matters Action Network website in early September 2009 called EmailChecker.org, "to counter conservative misinformation gone viral." It was initially focused on health care, but quickly changed to provide users with "ready-made responses to the most common and most egregious email memes," including responses to Mark Lloyd critics.

Media Matters Action Network can generate thousands of responses to its calls for action in just a few days.

Rabin-Havt's outfit is the 501(c)(4) lobbying companion group of Media Matters for America, a Web-based, tax-exempt, 501(c)(3) liberal research and information center with 2007 revenues of $8.7 million, "dedicated to comprehensively monitoring, analyzing, and correcting conservative misinformation in the U.S. media."

Media Matters for America has received 115 foundation grants totaling $10,985,000 since 2003.

The Media Matters founder, president and CEO is David Brock ($259,336 salary, $13,725 benefits). Brock is a former reporter for the conservative magazine *The American Spectator* who realized there was more money on the left, and said all his past writings critical of liberal figures were lies and slanders. He started his new group in 2003 to "set the record straight."

Seeing the value of a smart turncoat, John Podesta provided Brock with office space for his fledgling enterprise at the Center for American Progress and introduced him to the money.

Podesta and Brock attended a gathering in New York City put together by New Democrat Network officer Erica Payne to see a screening of *The Conservative Message Machine Money Matrix,* Rob Stein's alarming PowerPoint presentation that showed how conservatives came to dominate American politics and culture. The money was in the room with Brock: George Soros, insurance mogul Peter Lewis, wealthy psychologist Gail Furman, and New Jersey governor Jon Corzine.

That meeting spawned Stein's Democracy Alliance, funded by most of the people in the room (and many other wealthy liberals). Brock, the "King of Switcheroo," got quite a bit of the Democracy Alliance's money because his Media Matters treasurer was also on the board of the Democracy Alliance: Rachel Pritzker Hunter of the Hyatt Hotel Pritzkers. And another of Brock's board members was Jonathan Lewis, son of tycoon Peter Lewis.

Thirty of Media Matters' staff get over $50,000 a year salary, five of them over $100,000. Money, money, money.

Podesta also introduced Brock to the Tides Foundation, which funneled Media Matters $100,000 from software millionaire Stephen M. Silberstein, and $122,000 from an anonymous donor in 2003. The next year, Tides funneled over $2.1 million from a roster of affluent donors. Because Tides does not always reveal its donors, we don't know which of the following sent their money for Media Matters through Tides, but we do know they sent money:

- Leo Hindery Jr., a former cable magnate;

- Susie Tompkins Buell, co-founder of Esprit clothing company and close ally of Secretary of State Hillary Clinton;

- James Hormel, heir to the SPAM fortune;

- Bren Simon, a Democrat activist and the wife of shopping-mall developer Mel Simon;

- New York psychologist and philanthropist Gail Furman (mother of Jason Furman, Obama campaign advisor);

- Peter Lewis, insurance mogul (chairman of Progressive Corporation).

You get the idea. Mark Lloyd has friends – a huge, rich and well-linked existing netwar network. Half a day on the phone and you've mobilized an activist army just itching to get rid of those conservative talk shows.

And that's for a letter. Imagine the response when activists can draw blood and shut down one conservative talk radio station after another with just an email or a phone call or a letter to the FCC.

The problem with the Fairness Doctrine isn't the Fairness Doctrine.

It's the army of left-wing activists just waiting to be mobilized for revenge.

There are few things, I think, more frightening in the American mind than dark-skinned black men. Here I am.

The voice of the new FCC.

Whack!

CZAR WARS

![bar]

Nobody ever heard of Ernest Hemingway's 1920 detective story, *The Ash Heel's Tendon*, because it wasn't published until twenty-four years after the Nobel-winning writer died in 1961.

It flickered to life briefly when the *New York Times Magazine* ran it in 1985 – it wasn't very good, just an example of Hemingway's earliest work dug up by a literary historian.

Then it vanished for another twenty-four years.

But in mid-2009, a single part of a single line from *The Ash Heel's Tendon* gained huge fame when it flooded online dictionaries as an example of the word "czar."

Czar noun: A person having great power; an autocrat: *"the square-jawed, ruddy complacency of Jack Farrell, the czar of the Fifteenth Street police station" (Ernest Hemingway)*.

Conservative and libertarian bloggers soon copied the whole thing, Hemingway quote and all, with no idea where it came from (who cares?), and millions read it, then went on to what they were really looking for, the new definition of "czar:"

> Czar *informal:* An appointed official having special powers to regulate or supervise an activity: *a race-track czar; an energy czar.*

The czar of the Fifteenth Street police station.

Hemingway may have squirmed in his grave, but his simple,

vivid image hit a political nerve with Americans almost ninety years after he wrote it.

It was just exactly the image that disgusted – and alarmed – people about Obama's arrogant army of unelected, unaccountable meddlers into every corner of their lives.

The czar of this, the czar of that – petty and threatening at the same time – perfectly pictured by Hemingway's square-jawed, complacent czar of a precinct cop shop!

The czar of the Fifteenth Street police station.

That's so Obama.

What stupid, intrusive, self-important czar would he dream up next?

The czar of toilet paper control?

Obama was well aware of the public mood about his extravagant political appointments: he tried to lighten things up by joking at a broadcast awards dinner that a TV network could do a special from the White House called "Dancing With the Czars."

Mike Huckabee, former Arkansas governor and now television commentator for *ABC* and *Fox News*, matched him with a parody called, "Twinkle, Twinkle Little Czar ... I can't believe you're going to make my car."

Main Street America was not amused. As early as April, "tea party" demonstrations had erupted nationwide to protest Obama's takeover of the economy with his stimulus packages, bank bailouts, plans to overhaul the healthcare system, and restrictions on greenhouse gas emissions, supposedly to prevent global warming.

The "Tea Party" groups, of course, took the mantle of the American Revolution's Boston Tea Party, where disgruntled colonists dressed as Indians threw a cargo of imported English tea into the harbor to protest oppressive taxes.

But the 21st Century version was not really a tax protest, it was resentment that Obama was turning American democracy into socialism – and the "czars" were a standout symbol of his transformation.

They were too reminiscent of old-style Soviet commissars who controlled everything in the USSR, and sounded too much like the modern European Union's executive body, the European

Commission, which is unelected and unaccountable to any member state, and takes no instruction from any national government in the EU, yet wields executive power over all.

The Obama administration's 'Czar' appointments made headlines throughout the summer. First it was the resignation of 'Green Jobs Czar' Van Jones after exposure of his radical ties. Then came the revelation of openly gay "Safe Schools Czar" Kevin Jennings, back when he was a high school teacher, advising an underaged boy who was having sexual relations with an older man, "I hope you knew enough to use a condom." As if that wasn't scandalous enough, someone found his foreword to the 1999 book, *Queering Elementary Education: Advancing the Dialogue about Sexualities and Schooling*, which challenged readers to put gay-tolerance lessons in elementary schools.

That left the public concerned with the need for congressional oversight of such bizarre way-left executive appointments.

Enough was enough.

On Saturday, September 12, 2009, tens of thousands of Tea Party supporters streamed from all points in the country to a "March on Washington."

When they assembled, the line of protesters spread across Pennsylvania Avenue for blocks, all the way from the White House to the U.S. Capitol, according to the D.C. Homeland Security and Emergency Management Agency.

The White House was stunned.

A spokesman for D.C. Fire and Emergency Medical Services estimated the crowd was "in excess of 75,000," but aerial photos indicated it was at least 200,000 in the foreground, with a top estimate by organizers of 1.7 million, counting the photo background toward the Washington Monument and side streets. Critics said it wasn't over 100,000.

Liberals no doubt estimated low, conservatives high. That's politics.

It was a big crowd no matter how you count it. They waved U.S. flags and signs reading "Go Green - Recycle Congress" and "I'm Not Your ATM."

They chanted, "Enough! Enough!"

They carried signs with slogans such as "Obamacare makes

me sick," "It will kill you," and "If you think health care is expensive now, wait til it's 'free'."

A more overtly heated anti-Obama sign said, "Parasite In Chief." An over-the-top poster depicted the president above the slogan "I've Changed," sporting a moustache made famous by Nazi dictator Adolph Hitler. That was tasteless, but the guy carrying it had a dozen or more helpers trying to raise it with him, kind of like that famous World War II picture of four soldiers raising the American flag on Iwo Jima's Mount Suribachi.

Some protesters wore colonial costumes as they listened to speakers who warned of "judgment day" – Election Day 2010.

The March on Washington was organized across the country by several groups, including FreedomWorks Foundation, led by former House Majority Leader Dick Armey, Heartland Institute, Americans for Tax Reform, and the Ayn Rand Center for Individual Rights.

Czars weren't high on the agenda of most speakers, but the general hostility of the movement toward the Obama administration quickly sent the issue into the headlines anyway.

News reports, blogs and TV pundits dug into how "czars" had come to mean a presidential appointee.

One commentator said the term dates back to the Coolidge years.

Another pointed out that no official in American government holds an official title of czar for this or that.

Another said, "I should note that while the term czar has taken on a somewhat negative connotation in the media in the past few months, several presidents, including President Obama, have used the term themselves to describe the people they have appointed."

In a surprise move, not long after the anti-Obama march on Washington, liberal Democrat Senator Russell D. Feingold of Wisconsin released a letter asking the President to detail the roles and responsibilities of all of the czars in his administration and to explain why he believes the use of czars is consistent with the Senate's constitutional power to offer advice and consent on top-level executive branch officials.

Feingold is chairman of the Senate Judiciary Subcommittee on the Constitution.

His letter began by taking constitutional law professor Barack Obama to school on the Constitution:

> The Constitution gives the Senate the duty to oversee the appointment of Executive officers through the Appointments Clause in Article II, section 2. The Appointments Clause states that the President "shall nominate, and by and with the advice and consent of the Senate, shall appoint ambassadors, *other public ministers and consuls,* judges of the Supreme Court, *and all other officers of the United States,* whose appointments are not herein otherwise provided for, and which shall be established by law." This clause is an important part of the constitutional scheme of separation of powers, empowering the Senate to weigh in on the appropriateness of significant appointments and assisting in its oversight of the Executive Branch.

Feingold also asked the president's legal advisers to explain how their appointments square with the Constitution's mandate that the Senate oversee executive appointments.

"I hope that this information will help address some of the concerns that have been raised about new positions in the White House and elsewhere in the Executive Branch."

His letter also stressed that the czar issue was raised by his constituents in Wisconsin at several town hall meetings.

Feingold wasn't the only Democrat to voice concerns about czars.

California Senator Dianne Feinstein said that there needs to be better Senate oversight, although she was quick to add that some critics have incorrectly labeled a number of Senate-confirmed administration officials as White House czars – a technical quibble that many saw as a way to deflect criticism of Obama.

"If you look over certain people with real titles and real authority, I don't think it's quite fair to call, for example, David Hayes at the Department of Interior, a czar," the California Democrat said. "He's the deputy secretary of the Department of

Interior, and he's got real authority."

Feinstein said she thinks it's a "problem" when the White House appoints someone to a position that is not clearly defined. "I don't know what a car czar does, for example."

The late Senator Robert Byrd of West Virginia, a fierce defender of congressional authority, argued that the czars may upset checks and balances in the federal government.

Republicans on the Hill picked up on the czar issue, using them as a powerful symbol for the problems of unchecked government.

Republican Senator John Thune of South Dakota said the fight was a "great issue because it raises the whole issue of this agenda of expansion of government in Washington — and lack of accountability and transparency.

"It seems like everything we're doing right now is just consolidating power here, as opposed to distributing, which most of our folks would be more favorably disposed to, at least philosophically."

Republican Senator Lamar Alexander of Tennessee, who spearheads messaging for the Senate Republican Conference, said, "I just think it upsets the checks and balances. And it's a symbol of too many Washington takeovers."

Then the gun rights movement got involved.

The Second Amendment Foundation and Citizens Committee for the Right to Keep and Bear Arms, along with dozens of other pro-gun organizations became deeply worried about one of Obama's czars who seemingly had nothing to do with guns.

Cass R. Sunstein is a Harvard Law School professor and the head of the White House Office of Information and Regulatory Affairs in the Obama administration.

That makes him the "regulatory czar," but his long personal belief in animal rights and support of gun control raised fears that he's really using his power to become the "gun czar."

Sunstein has written 35 *books* that reveal a legal mind far to the left of the mainstream, and gave activists the ammunition to fight back with if he crosses the line into anti-gun extremism.

For example, Sunstein believes in regulating hunting out of existence. He told a Harvard audience in 2007 that "we ought to ban hunting." And in his book *The Rights of Animals: A Very Short Primer* (2002), he said:

> "I think we should go further...the law should impose further regulation on hunting, scientific experiments, entertainment, and (above all) farming to ensure against unnecessary animal suffering. It is easy to imagine a set of initiatives that would do a great deal here, and indeed European nations have moved in just this direction. There are many possibilities."

What "possibilities?" In Sunstein's world, animals should have just as many rights as people – *and they should be able to sue humans in court!*

"We could even grant animals a right to bring suit without insisting that animals are persons, or that they are not property," Sunstein said on page 11 of *Animal Rights: Current Debates and New Directions* (2004).

Picture this absurd hypothetical: you're returning from a successful hunting trip in doe season, only to find out that Regulatory Czar Cass Sunstein has subpoenaed you for killing your prize. You go to court. Can't you just see Bambi weeping on the witness stand at your trial for murdering his Mom? And how does your lawyer cross-examine a deer?

Seriously, what would that do to gun-owner rights? And jurisprudence?

Sunstein is a law professor. What does he think about the Second Amendment?

In *Radicals in Robes: Why Extreme Right-Wing Courts are Wrong for America* (2005), Sunstein says: "Almost all gun control legislation is constitutionally fine.... [O]n the Constitution's text, fundamentalists should not be so confident in their enthusiasm for invalidating gun control legislation."

A videotape of a lecture Sunstein gave at the University of Chicago on Oct. 23, 2007, shows him saying: "My coming view is that the individual right to bear arms reflects the success of an extremely aggressive and resourceful social movement and has much less to do with good standard legal arguments than it appears."

What about the handgun ban in the District of Columbia? He ridiculed anyone who would say, a "trigger lock interferes with his efforts at self-defense against criminals. What on Earth does that have to do with the Second Amendment as originally understood? My tentative suggestion is that the individual right to have guns as it's being conceptualized now is best taken as a contemporary creation and a reflection of current fears – not a reading of civic-centered founding debates."

Senator Saxby Chambliss (R-GA), a strong supporter of the Second Amendment, objected to Sunstein's nomination and put a hold on it, preventing him from being unanimously confirmed. The senator asked for an explanation. In an attempt to get Sen. Chambliss to remove his hold, Sunstein answered him:

> "I strongly believe that the Second Amendment creates an individual right to possess and use guns for purposes of both hunting and self-defense. I agree with the Supreme Court's decision in the *Heller* case, clearly recognizing the individual right to have guns for hunting and self-defense. If con-firmed, I would respect the Second Amendment and the individual right that it recognizes."

Based on those no-wiggle-room assurances, Senator Chambliss removed his hold and Sunstein was confirmed by the Senate in a 57-40 vote.

Did he really make such an instant turnaround about gun rights?

Maybe so, maybe not. Sunstein is a contributing editor to left-wing periodicals *The New Republic* and the George Soros-funded *American Prospect.* There's good reason to doubt him.

But the Senate confirmed Sunstein as regulatory czar – let's use the word that Senator Feinstein said wasn't fair, but that Main Street America understands all too well.

Millions of American gun owners were more than a little con-cerned about a czar with such an anti-gun mentality who had real authority – even perhaps some of that "murky, undefinied" authority that could turn "regulation" into "gun control" with "many possibilities."

Back on Capitol Hill, Senator Feingold got no answer to his letter. That annoyed him enough that he called a hearing of his

Constitution Subcommittee in early October, titled, "Examining the History and Legality of Executive Branch 'Czars'."

At the same time, public outrage and fear of Obama's czars heightened as *Fox News* – and talk show host Glenn Beck in particular – targeted them mercilessly.

It was the perfect buildup for a Czar Hearing.

Two of them, in fact. Shortly after the Feingold hearing, Democrat Joe Lieberman, chairman of the Senate Committee on Homeland Security and Governmental Affairs, became so angered at the White House he held his own hearing on the proliferation of policy 'czars' throughout the Obama Administration.

The first hearing was sharp-edged, but a little disappointing.

As Chairman Feingold noted in his opening statement, "historically a czar is an autocrat, and it's not surprising that some Americans feel uncomfortable about supposedly all-powerful officials taking over areas of the government. While there is a long history of the use of White House advisers and czars, that does not mean we can assume they are constitutionally appropriate."

Ranking Member Tom Coburn (R-OK) wondered aloud how much leeway Kenneth Feinberg, the "executive pay czar," would have to refuse an appearance before Congress.

Czar Feinberg had just announced that he was taking aim at compensation, and would "cut annual cash salaries for many of the top private sector employees under his authority."

Coburn surmised that since Feinberg acted under the auspices of the Treasury Department, he would be answerable to the Senate – probably.

Witnesses at the hearing included:

- T.J Halstead, Deputy Assistant Director of the Congressional Research Service;

- John C. Harrison and Tuan Samohan, law professors from the University of Virginia and Villanova University;

- Bradley H. Patterson, Jr., Author of *To Serve a President* (2008); and

- Matthew Spaulding, Director of the B. Kenneth Simon Center for American Studies.

Notably absent were any witnesses from the White House, despite an invitation from Senator Feingold.

Was that constitutional?

The senator took a swipe at Anita Dunn, Obama's communications director, who had used the White House blog to attack Glenn Beck for criticizing a list of 32 Obama czars.

Senator Feingold said, "The White House seems to want to fight the attacks against it for having too many 'czars' on a political level rather than a substantive level. I don't think that's the right approach. If there are good answers to the questions that have been raised, why not give them instead of attacking the motives or good faith of those who have raised questions?"

Then he announced that just the day before the hearing, the White House had actually sent him a weak effort to respond to his letter – barely giving him time to read it and distribute copies to committee members, staff, and witnesses for the hearing.

Greg Craig, the White House counsel, sent a three-page letter reviewing 18 positions within the administration that had been questioned, not only by Senator Feingold's letter, but also by a group of six Republican senators in their own letter.

Mr. Craig wrote that duties of many of the aides indeed come under the purview of congressional oversight, because they actually work within federal agencies whose employees have testified before Congress and whose records are public. Mr. Craig contended that some exercise no independent legal authority in their roles as presidential advisers.

None, he argued, "raise valid concerns about accountability, transparency or congressional oversight."

Craig did cede one point: "It is true that the president has created a small number of new White House positions to assist him in addressing matters of great public concern, in critical areas such as the environment and health care."

Those two high-profile positions were singled out by the expert witnesses.

Matt Spaulding questioned the role played by Carol Browner, the climate change/environment czar, in developing the EPA's new emissions standards, following a Supreme Court decision that CO_2 was a pollutant and could be regulated under the Clean Air Act.

Was that constitutional?

"As the number of czars expands," Spalding said, "the president's policy staff grows. There are more and more individuals acting more and more like administrative heads rather than advisers. That raises the possibility of political influence over decision-making.

"So I conclude that we have a dilemma with the current Congress giving away large amounts of authority. For instance, in the TARP bill, Congress gave the secretary of the Treasury extensive delegation of power, $700 billion to purchase troubled assets. Lo! and behold, we now own General Motors, and we have a 'car czar.'"

Was that constitutional?

Significantly, witnesses defended the President's right to appoint advisors, quoting the same Article II, Section 2, of the Constitution that Senator Feingold quoted to President Obama. The next clause in that section says:

> But the Congress may by Law vest the Appointment of such inferior Officers, as they think proper, in the President alone, in the Courts of Law, or in the Heads of Departments.

Then the question remained: had Congress passed any law that covered each of Obama's appointed Czars? Or was Obama just making up his own Constitution?

That was questionable. What about the well-publicized National Endowment of the Arts' conference call asking artists to support the President as a blatant misuse of authority.

Was that constitutional?

What about the negotiations between auto industry leaders and "Climate Czar" Carol Browner in which she told industry executives to "put nothing in writing."

Her appointed authority could be "dodging traditional constitutional requirements," Spaulding noted. "In addition to seeming to be beyond congressional legislative intent, it also seems to circumvent the authority of the EPA administrator," he said.

Was that constitutional?

That's how Senator Feingold's entire hearing went: all the testimony seemed to say that with today's massive government bureaucracy, just who is holding the real reins of policy is baffling.

It ended with nothing settled.

At the next White House briefing, Obama's Press Secretary, Robert Gibbs, dismissed the hearing with an insult: "I would assume that Congress and Senator Feingold have more weighty topics to grapple with than something like this."

Gibbs' bald assertion that constitutional issues of Senate oversight were of no consequence to the White House infuriated many senators

The Obama administration continued to slap the Senate in the face anyway.

"Health Care Czar" Nancy-Ann DeParle was granted the power to "develop and implement strategic initiatives" by an Executive Order personally signed by Obama.

Within two weeks, Democrat Joe Lieberman, chairman of the Senate Committee on Homeland Security and Governmental Affairs, became so angered at the White House that he held his own hearing on Obama's policy 'czars.'

Senator Lieberman's hearing was titled, "Presidential Advice and Senate Consent: The Past, Present, and Future of Policy Czars," its witnesses included:

- Former Assistant to the President for Homeland Security and Secretary of Homeland Security, Tom Ridge.
- George Mason University professor, Dr. James P. Pfiffner.
- Former Attorney-Advisor in the Office of Legal Counsel at the U.S. Department of Justice, Lee A. Casey.

- Former specialist in American National Government at the Congressional Research Service, Dr. Harold C. Relyea.

Chairman Lieberman opened the hearing with the pointed statement, "The Administration's Czars are invested with massive amounts of power and lack any level of congressional oversight. Without oversight, many of the czars are shrouded in a veil of secrecy, threatening the government transparency required for an effective democracy."

Ranking Committee Member Susan M. Collins (R-Maine) stressed that "oversight ensures the accountability and transparency our Founding Fathers envisioned."

She brought up the practical problem created by Obama's complex system of policy-advisors and czars: unlike Cabinet-level leaders, who hold clearly defined and Senate confirmed positions, the various presidential czars hold positions of murky, undefined power.

This leaves Congress and the public in the dark when it comes to who is really calling the shots, and as Senator Collins noted, undermined the "promises Obama made to the American people."

Lieberman's witnesses were more directly critical of President Obama.

Former Homeland Security Secretary Tom Ridge argued against presidential dependence on policy czars, saying they violate the fundamental spirit of the Constitution.

Ridge caustically noted that the President can evade congressional oversight by giving a czar authority that already belongs to another official, which is arguably the case with:

- Paul Volcker, head of the Economic Recovery Advisory Board, whose duties overlap the Treasury Secretary;
- Nancy Ann deParle, White House Office of Health Reform advisor, whose duties overlap the Health and Human Services Secretary; and

- Carol Browner, White House Office of Energy and Climate Change Policy advisor, whose duties greatly overlap those of the Environmental Protection Agency's Administrator.

Is that constitutional?

Senator Collins specifically pointed to both the Bush and Obama Administrations' appointments of 'Weapons of Mass Destruction Czars' as a complete circumvention of the WMD Officer position that was created by Congress in 2007.

The WMD Officer was ordered by Congress "To provide for the implementation of the recommendations of the National Commission on Terrorist Attacks Upon the United States. " The WMD Officer requires the same oversight required of all statutory officers.

But, to avoid this pesky check on the presidency, President Obama simply neglected to fill the congressionally created office, and created his own – "Special Assistant to the President and White House Coordinator for Arms Control and Weapons of Mass Destruction, Proliferation, and Terrorism."

For Obama to leave a statutory office vacant and instead announce his own Czar – who is to carry out the exact same duties – is a clear circumvention of Congressional oversight.

That left everyone in the hearing room with the uneasy feeling that the Senate was faced with a rogue president.

Finally, witness James Pfiffner brought up more threats to congressional constitutional authority:

- Presidential signing statements "that imply that the president may not faithfully execute the law;"
- Secret programs "that effectively nullify or circumvent the laws;"
- The President's use of the state secrets privilege "to avoid the disclosure of or accountability for their actions."

Senator Lieberman's hearing not only failed to settle anything, but also raised the anxiety level about the constitutionality of President Barack Obama's entire behavior.

What does the Senate do about a rogue president?

The unprecedented proliferation of czars made it crucial that the issue be dealt with sooner rather than later.

But how?

If a president will not obey the Senate, what do you do about it?

Defending the proper system of checks and balances is a necessity if the United States is to preserve the accountability and transparency required for a successful democracy.

With a rogue president in office, do we have a successful democracy?

Power, it's all about power.

Whack!

10

ACORN and Obama

"I come out of a grassroots organizing background. That's what I did for three and half years before I went to law school. That's the reason I moved to Chicago was to organize. So this is something that I know personally, the work you do, the importance of it. I've been fighting alongside ACORN on issues you care about my entire career. Even before I was an elected official, when I ran Project Vote voter registration drive in Illinois, ACORN was smack dab in the middle of it, and we appreciate your work."

- Barack Obama to ACORN leaders, November 2007.

The local media in fourteen states had treated ACORN as a liberal "community organizing" group of petty criminals accused of voter fraud – that is, until Obama hired them.

But when a presidential candidate pays over $800,000 to questionable old cronies for weird-sounding services, it makes national headlines.

The *New York Times* reported that in February of 2008, the Obama campaign's Federal Elections Commission report showed an $832,598 payment to an ACORN affiliate, CSI (Citizens Services Inc.), for "staging, sound, lighting."

Staging, sound, and lighting?

Eight-hundred-thousand bucks for staging, sound, and lighting?

When Republicans suggested that the payment was actually for voter registration – a more normal job for CSI – the Obama campaign filed an amended FEC report saying that the payment had been "mislabeled," and that the money was actually for GOTV (get-out-the-vote) efforts.

Then it was pointed out that ACORN had endorsed Obama for president in February 2008, about the same time Obama's campaign paid all that money to ACORN.

Obama ran quickly and quietly away from ACORN.

We'll lie and cheat until we're caught, is that the Obama message?

It certainly seems to be the message for the Association of Community Organizations for Reform Now (you can see why we just call it ACORN). The Wikipedia entry says:

> ACORN is a collection of community-based orga-
> nizations in the United States that advocate for
> low- and moderate-income families by working
> on neighborhood safety, voter registration, health
> care, affordable housing, and other social issues.
> ACORN has over 400,000 members and more than
> 1,200 neighborhood chapters in over 100 cities
> across the U.S., as well as in Argentina, Canada,
> Mexico, and Peru. ACORN was founded in 1970 by
> Wade Rathke and Gary Delgado. Maude Hurd has
> been National President since 1990; Bertha Lewis
> was appointed CEO in 2008.

House Judiciary Committee Chairman John Conyers Jr., Democrat of Michigan, said ACORN needed to be investigated.

Rep. Conyers was disturbed by a hearing he held in March, 2009 on voting issues in the 2008 presidential election. He heard testimony that shocked him.

Pittsburgh lawyer Heather Heidelbaugh, a member of the Republican National Lawyers Association executive committee, accused ACORN of voter fraud by helping unqualified voters to register, violating tax, campaign-finance and other laws – and even obtaining a list from the Barack Obama campaign that ACORN could use to solicit Democrat donors for a get-out-the-vote drive.

Heidelbaugh also testified that ACORN provided liberal causes with protest-for-hire services and coerced donations from targets of demonstrations through a mob-style shakedown it called the "muscle for the money" program.

Chairman Conyers was so appalled that he proposed holding hearings exclusively investigating ACORN's activities.

Things got worse.

When the Minority Staff of the U.S. House of Representatives' Committee on Oversight and Government Reform investigated the scandal, they called ACORN a "criminal enterprise."

Ranking minority member Darrell Issa, Republican of California, released an 88-page report in July 2009 that called ACORN a "criminal enterprise" that "uses its complex organizational structure to facilitate fraudulent and illegal acts," and listed 361 different exempt and non-exempt ACORN entities so confusing that even ACORN executives don't understand them all.

The allegations in the report dealt primarily with an embezzlement scandal.

According to a July 9, 2008 article in the *New York Times*, Dale Rathke, the brother of ACORN's founder, Wade Rathke, "embezzled nearly $1 million from ACORN and affiliated charitable organizations in 1999 and 2000."

The *Times* reported Dale Rathke embezzled $948,607.50, "carried as a loan on the books of Citizens Consulting Inc. ("CCI"), which provides bookkeeping, accounting and other financial management services to ACORN and many of its affiliated entities."

ACORN "chose to treat the embezzlement of nearly $1 million eight years ago as an internal matter and did not even notify its board."

That's bold – they failed to disclose the theft for eight years. Dale Rathke remained on ACORN's payroll until June 2008, when news broke of his wrongdoing.

Things got worse.

In early September, the Census Bureau severed its ties with ACORN, whose members had been hired to do canvassing during the 2010 census.

"We do not come to this decision lightly," Census director Robert Groves wrote in a letter to ACORN. "It is clear that ACORN's affiliation with the 2010 census promotion has caused sufficient concern in the general public, has indeed become a distraction from our mission, and may even become a discouragement to public cooperation, negatively impacting 2010 census efforts."

Then there was the matter of the whorehouses.

A few days after the Census Bureau rebuff, it was announced that four ACORN employees at its Baltimore, Washington, D.C., and Brooklyn offices were caught on video and later fired for helping a supposed prostitute and her pimp get loans for their dream houses of ill repute.

The "prostitute" was actually Hannah Giles, 20, a minister's daughter studying journalism at Florida International University, and the "pimp" was actually James O'Keefe, 25, who earned a degree in philosophy from Rutgers and is now a Fordham MBA student from New Jersey.

Both, said the *New York Post*, are "conservatives determined to expose what he sees as the hypocrisies and moral lapses of liberals by employing their own tactics against them."

O'Keefe and Giles funded the project themselves. This kind of undercover, guerrilla tactic is the "future of investigative journalism and political activism," O'Keefe said.

The real kicker is that the pair was inspired by Saul Alinsky's *Rules for Radicals*, the same thing that inspired Barack Obama in 1985 Chicago. Even though more often associated with the left, Alinsky's tactics are obviously a double-edged sword that cuts both ways.

O'Keefe said "If you can make impossible demands on your enemy, you can destroy them." He wanted to target and expose the "absurdities of the enemy by employing their own rules and language."

So he began using a hidden camera "in a location I'd rather not disclose" and started visiting offices around the Northeast.

O'Keefe first made a set of videos in 2008, in which Planned Parenthood employees agreed to earmark his donations for the abortions of African-American babies.

He was appalled that they agreed, but the experience led him to expect that ACORN might yield maybe "a few gotcha moments."

In reality, some ACORN employees were eager to dispense advice on playing the system and skirting the law.

"We never imagined they would all comply," O'Keefe said. "It's just disgusting they didn't just throw us out of the office," he said. A few actually did throw them out, but at locations in the Western U.S. On the East Coast, it was different.

O'Keefe and Giles bought garish clothing like a stereotypical pimp and prostitute in the movies. O'Keefe decked himself out in flamboyant flesh-peddler fur coat couture, and Giles, who went by the name "Eden," wore almost nothing.

Then they began visiting ACORN offices and asking for help setting up a whorehouse.

The ACORN workers were not the slightest bit judgmental or put off by the request for help in getting financing for a brothel.

Milagros Rivera, ACORN's Brooklyn office administrator, came the closest, and advised Giles, "don't get caught – it's against the law what you are doing, and there's a chance you'll get caught."

Another counselor told them, "You know, what goes on in the house we don't care. We just help you with the mortgage."

It's worth noting that ACORN's long history of not caring who they dealt with and "just helping you with the mortgage" – mortgages that ACORN knew would never be paid off – played a significant role in the home foreclosure disaster of 2008-2009.

But back to the adventures of nearly naked Giles and snazzy dresser O'Keefe:

> "Honesty is not going to get you the house," a loan counselor told them. "You can't say what you do for a living."

Another counselor told Giles to list her occupation as "performance artist," and even offered advice on how to claim as dependants underage girls recruited from Latin America for the business – one of the ruses Giles and O'Keefe used to find out how low ACORN would go.

Counselor Volda Albert freely offered financial advice to the young couple, and gave up on trying any moral advice.

"I can't tell you don't do it, because you won't listen to me," Albert said.

For tax and banking purposes, and to establish a legitimate income and credit history, Giles was told she needed to start saying she was a "freelancer."

"Don't say that you're a prostitute thing or whatever," she said.

Albert also suggested that Giles open two accounts at separate banks, depositing no more than $500 each a week to ensure few eyebrows are raised.

As for the rest of the money she earned from turning tricks, Albert told her to hide it away.

"When you buy the house with a back yard, you get a tin ... and bury it down in there, and you put the money right in, and you put grass over it, and you don't tell a single soul but yourself where it is," she said.

Albert even had advice on protecting O'Keefe from getting tied by authorities to Giles' prostitution. Her illegally obtained revenue could be given to O'Keefe through an intermediary, and then he could use it for a down payment on the house by applying for a "no doc" loan.

Before bidding them good luck, Albert offered two final suggestions.

"Save for a rainy day," she said. "And live well."

That did it. Shortly after Giles and O'Keefe released their embarrassing pimp-and-prostitute videos, the House of Representatives voted to deny any federal money to ACORN.

House Republicans added the prohibition on federal ACORN money to the Democrat bill on college lending. It was approved by a bipartisan vote of 345 to 75, and the Senate reaffirmed the move 85 to 11 on a prohibition added to an Interior Department bill, showing that Democrats also saw the political liability in ACORN.

Representative Eric Cantor of Virginia, the No. 2 House Republican, said, "ACORN has violated serious federal laws, and today the House voted to ensure that taxpayer dollars would no longer be used to fund this corrupt organization."

It was no small thing for ACORN: since 1994, the group had received an estimated $53 million in federal aid.

ACORN's chief executive, Bertha Lewis, put on her brave face and told reporters that the action would have little impact because most of the group's income comes from members and other supporters.

However she soon changed her tune. In early November, she said she "underestimated" the effect of the resolution. "It gave the green light for others to terminate our funds as well. All of our state and local grants were frozen, as were most of our private foundation funds."

ACORN filed a lawsuit in United States District Court in Brooklyn, asking that its federal financing be restored. The suit said that the House resolution constituted a "bill of attainder," or a legislative determination of guilt which punished them without benefit of a trial, which is a violation of the U.S. Constitution's Article 1, Section 9.

How's that for brassy?

The suit noted that several applications made by ACORN for contracts with federal agencies have also been rejected, including a bid for a $780,000 grant for outreach to poor communities about asthma and an application to set up public computer centers in five cities.

The lawsuit names as defendants Timothy F. Geithner, the Treasury secretary; Shaun Donovan, the secretary of Housing and Urban Development; and Peter R. Orszag, who, as the director of the Office of Management and Budget, enforced the freeze on financing, the suit alleges.

Michael C. Dorf, a Cornell University constitutional law professor, said lawsuits claiming that lawmakers have violated the constitutional prohibition on bills of attainder are difficult to win, because courts have found that the mere declaration that someone has committed a crime has meaning only if some punishment is ordered, which traditionally has meant forfeiture of property or government seizure of assets.

Dorf told the *New York Times* that, "Even though it's certainly plausible to infer, given the politics and timing, that there was an aim to punish ACORN, the government would undoubtedly defend on the grounds they can choose to fund or not to fund."

As if that wasn't bad enough, at nearly the same time as the lawsuit was filed, Louisiana Attorney General Buddy Caldwell raided ACORN's national headquarters in New Orleans and seized paper records and computer hard drives that some thought could lead to the White House.

A week later, President Obama appointed Bob Bauer – who had worked for Obama during his 2008 presidential campaign – as White House counsel.

That, said Rep. Steve King, Republican of Iowa, makes Bauer "perfectly positioned to be tasked with erasing the tracks between Obama and ACORN."

"Bob Bauer has a public record of defending Barack Obama's relationship with ACORN," King told supporters. "Bauer's hiring appears to be a tactical maneuver to strategically defend the White House from ACORN's misdeeds."

Obama's election campaign had flopped badly in erasing those tracks with its weasel-worded www.stopthesmears.com denials – because old newsletter, magazine and newspaper reports kept popping up with kind words for the candidate spoken years earlier by ACORN leaders praising his help.

Obama's past was catching up with him.

Obama's close ties to ACORN hinged on a decision he made before going to Harvard Law School – to return to Chicago and continue his community activism.

When his fellow editors voted him President of the *Harvard Law Review* in 1990, it not only made him an instant celebrity (for being the first black student elected to the position), but it almost guaranteed him a coveted clerkship with the U.S. Supreme Court after graduation and a lucrative offer from the law firm of his choice.

But he told the *New York Times* that after graduation the next year, he probably would go back to Chicago, spend two years at a corporate law firm to pay off his school loans, then look for community work.

"Down the road, he plans to run for public office," wrote *Times* reporter Tammerlin Drummond.

Nobody believed it. Passing up such grandiose, power-packed opportunities for a mediocre life in Chicago was unthinkable.

But two events made it easy for Obama to keep his promise to himself: he met a girl in his first summer job during law school and he got a book deal during his last year in law school.

In 1989, Barack Obama found a job as a "summer associate" at the elitist Sidley Austin law firm in Chicago. It was no accident. Sidley didn't usually hire first-year law students as summer associates, so there had to be a good reason for it.

On campus, Obama's research assistance on Tribe's *Curvature of Constitutional Space* and his selection as an editor on the *Harvard Law Review* created a lot of buzz. But it was Martha Minow, a law professor at Harvard, who told her father, Newton N. Minow, managing partner at Sidley, that Barack was possibly the most gifted student that she had ever taught, and got him the job.

Michelle Robinson, Harvard Law School graduate (1988), was assigned to mentor Obama through the intricacies of being a real-live hot-shot lawyer in a real-live hot-shot law firm. She felt annoyed by all the chattering about this guy with the weird name and Hawaiian origin. She expected some nerdy, over-intellectual snot, and was prepared to dislike him.

The *Washington Post* wrote of Michelle:

> "He sounded too good to be true," she told David Mendell, author of "Obama: From Promise to Power." "I had dated a lot of brothers who had this kind of reputation coming in, so I figured he was one of these smooth brothers who could talk straight and impress people. So we had lunch, and he had this bad sport jacket and a cigarette dangling from his mouth, and I thought: 'Oh, here you go. Here's this good-looking, smooth-talking guy. I've been down this road before.'"

She had come from a South Side Chicago family that lived in a one-bedroom, one bathroom apartment. She shared the divided-off living room with her older brother Craig. Her mother stayed home and her father, who had to use crutches because of multiple sclerosis, was still able to work operating a pumping station for the City. The two kids were both bright, both skipped the second grade, and attended only public schools until Craig went to Princeton University (and became basketball coach at Brown, and later Oregon State University), then Michelle followed him, graduated *cum laude* from Princeton (1985), and finished up with a *Juris Doctor* degree from Harvard Law School.

Obama unsuccessfully asked Michelle out several times at Sidley; she thought it would be "tacky" to date the only other black person in their division – there were half a dozen others in the firm, but not in their work area. She kept trying to fix him up with other girls, but he wasn't interested.

Halfway through summer, though, Michelle said okay.

The official story is that on the couple's first date Michelle agreed to spend the day with Barack. They went to the Chicago Art Institute, had lunch at an outdoor cafe, walked and talked, saw the newly released Spike Lee movie *Do the Right Thing*, and had a drink on the 99th floor of the John Hancock building.

Michelle told CNN, "We clicked right away ... by the end of that date it was over ... I was sold."

That may be too pat and over-rehearsed, but Newton Minow and his wife, Jo, told the *Washington Post* that they ran into the pair at the popcorn stand at a movie theater about that time. Minow is not sure, but thinks it may have been their fabled first date to see *Do the Right Thing*. "I think they were a little embarrassed," Minow said with a laugh.

Barack and Michelle became an item.

At summer's end, Obama went back to Harvard, where he was elected president of the *Harvard Law Review* in February. It merited a mention or two in a few wire service notices, but then it caught fire. As *GQ* correspondent Robert Draper wrote:

> A *New York Times* reporter hoofs it up to Cambridge, and his article, published February 6, 1990, is the first to describe the meanderings of the biracial Hawaiian who was now declaring Chicago his home. Among those taking note are several book publishers and a young woman

named Jane Dystel, who works in the Flatiron district with renowned literary agent Jay Acton, whose clients include James Baldwin, Tip O'Neill, and Sandinista leader Daniel Ortega. Acton says to Dystel, The guy could be another Baldwin— maybe we could get another *Fire Next Time* out of him. Dystel contacts Obama: There's a book in all this. Obama has thought about writing a novel but never a memoir. Still, he has student loans, so why not? Dystel helps him fashion a book proposal, she submits it to multiple publishers—and on November 28, 1990, the Simon & Schuster imprint Poseidon Press issues a six-figure contract to 29-year-old Barack Obama for a book tentatively titled *Journeys in Black and White*.

The six figures were $150,000. Ann Patty, editorial director at Poseidon, paid him half that right away. His due date for delivering the finished manuscript was June 15, 1992. But he didn't start writing. He had a law degree to finish and a few other things to do first.

One of them was to take eight days off to attend a Los Angeles national training course taught by the Industrial Areas Foundation, a course described by Ryan Lizza as "a station of the cross for Alinsky acolytes." He was moving not only up through law school, but also up through the ranks of recognized Alinsky gurus.

Obama kept on with his *Harvard Law Review* job and survived the celebrity with aplomb. His term was nothing spectacular: his volume today is not among the most cited in the Harvard Law Review canon – but it was creditable and workmanlike.

His unsigned *HLR* student note on the abortion issue is fairly standard, fairly dull material. A "student note" is a law review article written entirely by a student law review editor, sometimes signed, but the president's student note is traditionally unsigned, as was Obama's, which provoked a storm of ignorance from critics who claimed he never wrote anything in the *Harvard Law Review*.

Newton Minow got him an associate job in the summer of 1990 in Chicago at Hopkins & Sutter and Obama picked up things with Michelle.

And in the spring of 1991, he graduated *magna cum laude.*

Not bad for a half-white black guy from Hawaii with a weird name.

And now, with all the notoriety about being the first black *HLR* president, everybody wanted a piece of him.

Obama immediately received an offer of a clerkship with Federal Court of Appeals for the District of Columbia Circuit Judge Abner Mikva, a former Hyde Park congressman – but he turned it down.

As promised, Obama, law degree in hand, returned to Chicago and Michelle. But not the way he expected.

Obama didn't realize that he had made an important friend while president of the law review: a professor at the University of Chicago Law School named Michael W. McConnell submitted an article titled, "The Origins and Historical Understanding of Free Exercise of Religion," that landed in Obama's editing box.

Professor McConnell had a pretty good idea what would come back, but it didn't.

As McConnell later told *Politico*, "A frequent problem with student editors is that they try to turn an article into something they want it to be. It was striking that Obama didn't do that. He tried to make it better from my point of view."

McConnell, a conservative legal scholar who is now a federal appellate judge, was impressed enough to urge the University of Chicago Law School to seek Obama out as an academic prospect, which they did.

The faculty-appointments chair of Saul Alinsky's *Alma Mater*, Doug Baird, gave Obama a fellowship arranged by McConnell, including a stipend, an office on the sixth floor of the law school with a view onto the once lovely neighborhood of Woodlawn, devastated by the 1968 riots following Martin Luther King's assassination – and a computer to use for writing, not only the course materials for classes be was obligated to teach, but also for writing his much put-off book.

But first Obama went to see his old friends at the Developing Communities Project – Kellman, Kruglik, Galluzo, and Owens. He was welcomed as a conquering hero without the parade. And they immediately began thinking about what the newly minted lawyer might do, considering his duties at the university and the deadline on his book and the fact that he hadn't taken his state bar exam yet.

Lawyer and civil-rights activist Sandy Newman formed Project Vote in Washington, D.C. in 1985, pioneering such now-commonplace practices as registering people at food-stamp and welfare offices. He had long opted to avoid Illinois, even after the death of Harold Washington decimated the minority vote, saying, "The Democratic Party in Cook County still actively uses a bounty system for most registrations, and we don't wish to get associated with that."

But in 1991, Carol Moseley Braun, angered by Illinois' incumbent Democratic senator Alan Dixon's vote to confirm Clarence Thomas, challenged him in the March primary election and won an upset.

That changed Newman's feelings. Project Vote focused on minority voters, and on states where Newman felt they could explain to them why their vote matters. Braun made Illinois a target.

So Newman decided to open a Cook County Project Vote office and went looking for someone to head it.

By then it was March of 1992. Obama had settled into his university fellowship and was getting nowhere writing his book. What started as a treatment of voting rights had morphed into something resembling a memoir, he told Doug Baird at the university.

Newman told *Chicago Magazine*, "I was asking around among community activists in Chicago and around the country, and they kept mentioning the name Barack Obama,"

Newman says that Obama was then "working with church and community leaders on the West Side, and he was writing a book that the publisher Simon & Schuster had contracted for while he was editor of the law review. He was 30 years old."

He didn't mention the university fellowship because Obama had not spread that around.

When Newman called, Obama agreed to put his other work aside. "I'm still not quite sure why," Newman says. "This was not glamorous, high-paying work. But I am certainly grateful. He did one hell of a job."

And "ACORN was smack dab in the middle of it," as Obama told ACORN leaders in 2007.

At the same time, Obama was invited to join Davis, Miner, Barnhill & Galland, a law firm of 12 attorneys entrenched in Chicago politics and specializing in civil rights litigation and neighborhood economic development. Principal Judson Miner had been a close associate of the late Mayor Harold Washington and knew the local ACORN leaders well.

Obama accepted, but told them he wouldn't be available until early 1993 – he was writing a book and he would be leading the Project Vote registration campaign for six months, until October 1992, then needed some time to prep for the bar exam.

They said okay.

In April, Obama took over Newman's Chicago voter registration drive, set a goal of registering 150,000 of the 400,000 unregistered African Americans in the state, and quickly assembled a staff of ten reliable activists.

He began prowling his old stomping grounds, now equipped with high honors and a lot of important political contacts from his summer associate jobs. He recruited volunteers from every place he knew, black churches, community groups, and political campaigns. He had soon trained 700 deputy voter registrars (out of a total of 11,000 citywide), an uncounted number of them ACORN activists.

Then Obama went to Terri Gardner, president of black-owned Brainstorm Communications, to design a saturation media campaign. She came up with the group's slogan, "It's a Power Thing," which became ubiquitous in African-American neighborhoods.

You could just hear the echoes of long-dead Alinsky's voice shouting, "Power!"

It's a Power Thing posters went up in all 19 minority districts in town. Black-oriented radio stations aired the group's ads and announced where people could go to register.

Minority owners of McDonald's restaurants allowed registrars on site and donated paid radio time to Project Vote.

Labor unions provided funding. In late fall, the Clinton/ Gore campaign did too; their national voter-registration drive was being directed by Chicago alderman Bobby Rush.

It was a smash, the most successful grass-roots voter-registration campaign in Chicago's history at the time. It was credited with putting Carol Mosley Braun in the U.S. Senate.

"It was the most efficient campaign I have seen in my 20 years in politics," said Sam Burrell, alderman of the West Side's 29th Ward and a veteran of many registration drives.

Chicago ACORN leader Toni Foulkes wrote in the journal *Social Policy*, "Since then, we have invited Obama to our leadership training sessions to run the session on power every year, and, as a result, many of our newly developing leaders got to know him before he ever ran for office. Thus, it was natural for many of us to be active volunteers in his first campaign for State Senate and then his failed bid for U.S. Congress in 1996. By the time he ran for U.S. Senate, we were old friends."

When Obama finally joined up with Davis, Miner, Barnhill & Galland in 1993, one of the cases he won was representing ACORN in *Buycks-Roberson v. Citibank Federal Savings Bank*, in which ACORN pressed for Citibank to make more loans

to marginally qualified African-American applicants "in a race neutral way." Obama won a settlement of small amounts of cash or credit toward a mortgage application for his plaintiffs and legal fees of up to $950,000 for the lawyers.

He also represented ACORN in a successful lawsuit titled ACORN v. Edgar (Jim Edgar being the governor of Illinois at the time) against the state of Illinois to force state compliance with a federal voting access law, called "Motor Voter." He received the IVI-IPO Legal Eagle Award for it in 1995.

Crain's *Chicago Business* named Obama to its 1993 list of "40 under Forty" powers to be.

Later, as director of the Woods Fund and Chairman of the Board of Chicago Annenberg Challenge Obama helped steer funds to ACORN through various grants.

Make no mistake: Barack Obama is as much the President from ACORN as his worst critics say he is.

It's all about power.

Whack!

11

America at the Brink

What do we make of all this?

We used to live in a in a country that honored the rule of law.

With a Chicago mafia running the bureaucracy like it was the Socialist States of America, a Democrat-ridden Congress that seems hell-bent on turning us into a debt-ridden Third World economy, and an eloquent but indecisive Harvard Law graduate sitting in the Oval Office – what's in store for America?

We've seen the Obama Agenda for Congress mircd in public outcry.

Take Card Check, for example. That's the no-secret-ballot union organizing proposal that would allow employees to organize into a labor union if a majority signs authorization "cards" saying they want to be represented by the union.

Obama, while a Senator in 2007, was an original co-sponsor of the so-called "Employee Free Choice Act," and urged his colleagues to pass the bill:

> I support this bill because in order to restore a sense of shared prosperity and security, we need to help working Americans exercise their right to organize under a fair and free process and bargain for their fair share of the wealth our country

creates. The current process for organizing a work-
place denies too many workers the ability to do so.

Since everyone can see who signs a card, it's not a Card
Check, it's a Blank Check for union organizers to identify and
intimidate independent employees into joining or else. It sounds
so much like Alinsky's community organizing manual, *Rules for
Radicals*, it hardly needs pointing out.

Even a lot Democrats gagged on that one, so the bill went
nowhere.

The Health Care bill was amended so many times, and the
government-run "public option" was in and out so often that
the Democrat core constituency was furious at the president for
not taking a stronger stand for what he promised in his election
campaign.

Barack Obama must have been appalled that even the
blacks, gays, and starry-eyed, far-left activists who pushed him
over the electoral top deserted him.

His Climate Change bill and its disastrous cap-and-trade
scheme raised such public rage that the bill was quickly put on
the back burner. It was the last straw for the libertarians and
conservatives who never voted for Obama and brought the 1773
"Tea Party" rebellion up to date as a modern political powerhouse.

Obama's healthcare push cost him the Democrat superma-
jority in the Senate – and a big embarrassment when his visit
to Massachusetts to campaign for Martha Coakley couldn't save
her from being trounced by Scott Brown.

"Obama can't help you," became the mantra of Democrat
campaign advisors, prompting many incumbents to retire instead of facing a hopeless fight.

Think how fast Obama's approval rating fell from 67 percent
to 48 percent because of his generally poor performance.

So, whose president is he, anyway?

A disaffected ultra-left-wing professor of political science at
Hofstra University in New York – David Michael Green by name
– nailed Obama spot-on:

President Nothingburger.

But, as I have warned throughout this book, do not
underestimate Barack Obama.

He's very smart and he's very ruthless and he's very slippery.

He's like those scorching mudflows that slithered through the ridges and ravines of erupting Mount Saint Helens – if he can't just overwhelm an obstacle, he'll find a way around it.

Why I warn you again is this: Barack Obama has made a lot of laws you probably never heard of – and he made them without asking Congress.

He did it with Executive Orders.

That's an order issued by the president, head of the executive branch, and has *the full force of law* – in practical terms, anyway, since neither Congress nor the courts do much about them.

But critics have long complained that Executive Orders are a sneaky way for a president to exceed executive authority and get away with it.

Are they constitutional?

The Constitution's first sentence (after the Preamble) is, "All legislative power herein granted shall be vested in a congress of the United States, which shall consist of a senate and house of representatives."

No mention of the President or Executive Orders.

Article II of the Constitution says "the executive power shall be vested in a president of the United States of America." Read Section 3 and you'll see that it makes the president's job very clear: "He shall take care that the laws are faithfully executed."

Executed, not made.

Well, then, what about those Executive Orders that *have the force of law*?

Are they constitutional?

Some are, particularly those authorized by Acts of Congress, specifically delegating to the president some degree of discretionary power.

Some may not be, particularly those which the president merely claims to have authority by the power inherently granted to the executive by the Constitution.

In fact, the Constitution says nothing about the president giving orders to anybody except the military as commander-in-chief, to his department heads, and to order pardons and reprieves. He can make treaties, nominate ambassadors and consuls, and judges of the Supreme Court, but only with the approval of two-thirds of the Senate.

The rest is silence. Any other supposedly constitutional Presidential powers may be totally imaginary.

Lawsuits have challenged the legal validity behind specific Executive Orders without much luck.

It has also become commonplace for a president to issue an Executive Order only to have the next President revoke it.

Obama has done a lot of that with Executive Orders issued by President George W. Bush.

But the reason I'm talking about Executive Orders in this final chapter is that Barack Obama is using them to create a silent revolution inside the United States government.

He's not just fiddling around reorganizing departments or adding czars or shuffling duties or consolidating tasks or tinkering with regulations.

Yes, he's doing all that, but there's much more.

He's building an authoritarian engine to drive American policy (policy is supposed to be the job of Congress) and he's defining what the law means (judging legality is supposed to be the job of the courts).

Is that constitutional? No, it's not.

But the American system is presently arranged so that only nine people can tell you what's constitutional and what's not, and it only takes five of them to rule what's law and what's not. Getting to the Supreme Court is very expensive. The chances of even convincing them to hear your case, much less winning it, are dicey.

Barack Obama is pretty much free to do what he wants with Executive Orders.

Doing things with a smiling face and a stone-cold will is an Obama character trait. Remember, *New York Observer* writer Peter Kaplan told us that Obama was great *because he is cold* – he does things quietly, "no drama Obama," but works ruthlessly through others like the community organizer he is, and uses any means necessary to achieve larger goals.

Obama's Executive Orders are his best weapon, quiet, seemingly benign, even beneficial, until you question their impact. Consider a few:

- *January 11, 2010:* Establishing Council of Governors Purpose: The Council will review such matters as involving the National Guard of the various States; homeland defense; civil support; synchronization and integration of State and Federal military activities in the United States; and other matters. Question: How do you "synchronize and integrate" the military activities of the state and federal governments without compromising the sovereignty, rights, and chain of command of either one?

- *December 17, 2009:* International Organizations Immunities Purpose: To extend the appropriate privileges, exemptions, and immunities to the International Criminal Police Organization (INTERPOL).

Question: Why are we giving full diplomatic immunity to a law enforcement agency?

- December 09, 2009: Creating Labor-Management Forums Purpose: To create a nonadversarial forum for managers, employees, and employees' union representatives to discuss Government operations that will promote satisfactory labor relations and improve the productivity and effectiveness of the Federal Government. Question: Are union bosses telling federal officials what to do?

- October 05, 2009: Federal Leadership in Environmental, Energy, and Economic Performance Purpose: To require Federal agencies to set a 2020 greenhouse gas emissions reduction target; increase energy efficiency; reduce fleet petroleum consumption; conserve water; reduce waste; support sustainable communities; and leverage Federal purchasing power to promote environmentally-responsible products and technologies.

Question: What does that long list of generalities mean, exactly?

That last one, the October 5 Executive Order, deserves close scrutiny. It hides a morass of new powers for new bureaucracies that threatens the entire fabric of American society. It's the archetypal example of stone-cold Obama will carried out by others.

We'll give it the close scrutiny it needs as our parting shot, but we need to plant firmly in our minds that Mr. Nice-Guy Obama is really Obama the Cold.

So let's go back to follow his career one last time, and see clearly the cold, ruthless, any-means-necessary man behind the charming front.

After Barack Obama and Michelle Robinson began dating in the summer of 1989, they didn't see a lot of each other while Obama was back at Harvard. At the end of that fantastic school year as president of the Harvard Law Review, Obama's mentor, Newton Minow, got him a summer associate job in Chicago at Hopkins & Sutter – a law firm best known for its tax, insurance, and public policy work – and Obama picked up things with Michelle.

They talked about the Law Review and this Jane Dystel, an agent who thought he ought to write a book on race and voting rights that he wasn't sure he could write. And he didn't sound very interested in marriage. He even sounded like he didn't think the institution was meaningful in today's society.

Obama the Cold.

That was their first argument.

Obama went back for his last year at Harvard Law and returned to Chicago with a J.D. *magna cum laude* and a $150,000 book contract. He could have accepted Judge Mikva's offer of an appeals court clerkship or found a rich K Street law firm in Washington to give him a big salary.

But that's not the path to real power, not to the political power he told his Developing Communities buddies he wanted. He came back to Chicago to find his own path to power and to hook up again with Michelle Robinson.

Obama took her to dinner at a fancy restaurant where he launched into another of his endless diatribes about whether marriage still meant anything as an institution. Robinson lit into her cold boyfriend, lecturing him on the need to get serious in their relationship.

That put a crimp in things for some time.

Obama saw the Project Vote campaign as a step toward the power he wanted, finished that, and once he was ready to take the next step, convinced Michelle to go to dinner with him at Gordon's, the tony Chicago landmark restaurant on Clark Street. He promised not to argue with her about the meaning of marriage as an institution. She gave him an answer that amounted to "You better not."

They had a fine dinner.

When dessert came, on the plate was a box. Inside the box was an engagement ring.

Some years later, Michelle told the *Chicago Sun-Times*, "He said, 'That kind of shuts you up, doesn't it?'"

How Obama: That kind of shuts you up, doesn't it?

Michelle and Barack were married on October 3, 1992 by Rev. Jeremiah A. "God Damn America" Wright Jr. at Trinity United Church of Christ in Chicago, Illinois. The reception was held at the South Shore Cultural Center.

Then there's the book. Recall that in 1990, agent Jane Dystel had persuaded Poseidon, a small imprint of Simon & Schuster, to authorize a $150,000 advance for Obama's proposed book on racial voter rights. He missed the June 1992 deadline. Simon & Schuster canceled the contract, which probably meant that Obama had to pay back at least some of what he had received of the advance.

Without missing a beat, Dystel approached Henry Ferris, then a senior editor of Times Book at Random House. Ferris and publisher Peter Osnos met with Obama, found his story fascinating, and believed he would finish the book. They paid him another advance – $40,000.

Obama's half-sister, Maya Soetoro-Ng, said he retreated to Bali for several months with his wife, Michelle, "to find a peaceful sanctuary where there were no phones."

It later came out that Obama actually left Michelle behind and went to Bali alone – and they hadn't even been married a year.

Obama the Cold.

By then, his book on racial voter rights had morphed into a personal memoir, *Dreams from my Father*, not a sociological commentary titled *Journeys in Black and White* by a celebrity Harvard Law grad. He finally finished a spotty draft.

But he couldn't make it sound right. His law school training backfired on him: his sentences were too long and too matter of fact. It told the story, all right, but it didn't have the passion, the build-up, the stirring cadences, the dramatic climaxes and gripping images that he wanted. It sounded like a lawyer.

After Obama won the presidential election, *Politico* reporters Ben Smith and Jeffrey Resner read Obama's student note in the Harvard Law Review and observed that "the temperate legal language doesn't display the rhetorical heights that run through his memoir, published a few years later."

Obama knew that his book draft didn't have any lift. The best thing he had ever written was *Why Organize? Problems and Promise in the Inner City.* That was okay for a university periodical, but it didn't soar like a memoir should.

Neither did his first cut of *Dreams,* and the final book *had to* soar.

Many have thought that Obama must have had a ghostwriter – it was highly unlikely that a first-time author produced what *Time Magazine* later called "the best-written memoir ever produced by an American politician" (even though Obama wasn't yet a politician when he wrote it).

But Jack Cashill, Ph.D., a veteran analyst of intellectual fraud, and author of the sharp-eyed, sharp-tongued book, *Hoodwinked: How Intellectual Hucksters Hijacked American Culture*, happened to notice a bizarre coincidence.

Dreams from my Father sounded just like *Fugitive Days*, the 2001 memoir of Bill Ayers, co-founder of the Weather Underground, a self-described communist revolutionary group that conducted a campaign of bombing public buildings, including the U.S. Capitol, during the 1960s and 1970s. In 1980, Ayers turned himself in, was never convicted because of prosecutorial misconduct, never repented his crimes, and is now a professor in the College of Education at the University of Illinois at Chicago.

His wife, Bernadine Dohrn, was a leader of the Weather Underground, committed many bombing crimes, wrote a tract called, "Our Class Struggle," and as an avowed communist, said, "Marxism-Leninism is the most significant development in our recent history," but turned herself in with her husband, entered a guilty plea to charges of aggravated battery and bail jumping, served less than a year in jail, and is now an Associate Professor of Law at Northwestern University School of Law in Chicago.

Well, that's just Chicago. Making a point of it won't change anything – except public perception of President Barack Obama.

The resemblance between the books by Ayers and Obama was no coincidence. The Obamas are Hyde Park neighbors of Ayers and Dohrn. Other neighbors confirm that the two couples know each other well and that Obama and Ayers frequently worked together on projects.

Cashill went to work with linguistic analysis methods used to detect fraud. He picked similar passages from *Dreams From my Father* and *Fugitive Days* and compared their scores on reading ease and grade reading level. *Fugitive Days* scored a 54 on reading ease and a 12th grade reading level. *Dreams* scored a 54.8 on reading ease and a 12th grade reading level. Scores can range from 0 to 121, so hitting a nearly exact score matters.

Odd that Obama's 2008 political book, *Audacity of Hope*, averages more than 29 words a sentence and clocks in with a 9th grade reading level, three levels below *Dreams*.

Cashill tested for sentence length, a significant and telling factor. *Fugitive Days* averaged 23.13 words a sentence. *Dreams* averaged 23.36 words a sentence. That was too suggestive.

Cashill then commissioned an independent scientific comparative analysis. The experts he hired used a full range of technical methods, comparing style, word choices, set-phrases, images – oddly, Ayers had long experience at sea and used sea images in his book that also appear throughout Obama's book, although *Dreams* has nothing to do with the sea. The analysts all agreed that so many factors matched that the probability that Ayers had some role in Obama's book was so high as to be nearly certain.

Then author Christopher Andersen released his 2009 book, *Barack and Michelle: Portrait of an American Marriage*, and confirmed Cashill's highly-educated guess. With access to people Cashill did not have, Andersen wrote that when Barack was stumped by his not-so-great draft, Michelle suggested he seek the help of "his friend and Hyde Park neighbor Bill Ayers."

Andersen, quoting anonymous but knowledgeable sources that may have included Michelle herself, wrote that Obama had taped interviews with relatives to flesh out his family history, and those "oral histories, along with a partial manuscript and a truckload of notes, were given to Ayers."

Does it matter that Obama used a ghostwriter or "book doctor"?

No, it doesn't. Politicians nearly always use ghostwriters or collaborators for their book ventures. John McCain credited Mark Salter in his memoir, *Faith of My Fathers.*

Does it matter that Obama lied about it and said he didn't know Ayers very well and that he was just a guy who lived in the same neighborhood?

Yes, it does. Obama might have lost the election if such a close connection to such an unrepentant communist radical became clear and indisputable.

How could Obama win if it came out that communist terrorist Bill Ayers had inserted that poignant but phony story about young Obama in Punahou prep school staying up nights reading angry books by angry black writers that drove him to smoke dope as an escape – the story that his Punahou school friends later called "crap" and "bull."

But Obama didn't have to explain. Nobody knew anything then. So Obama made a bucket of money on it. The original 1995 printing only sold about 10,000 copies, but when Obama gave his knock-'em-dead speech as keynoter of the 2004 Democratic Convention in Boston, the book took off, selling about 500,000 copies. Counting all the royalties *Dreams* has earned from all its versions (Obama won a Grammy for his reading of the audio version), he netted about $1 million.

Cold Obama. It's all about power.

Whack!

The book business gets colder. When a new and bigger opportunity appeared, Obama showed his true colors. Just before he was sworn in as a U.S. Senator, Obama was offered and signed a two-book deal with Crown for "seven figures" ($1.5–$2.0 million, best guess, we may never know). By signing the contract before taking office, Obama didn't fall under disclosure and reporting rules for members of Congress.

Obama the Cold. It's all about power.

Whack!

But what tells us most about Obama the Cold is this: When the big Crown offer came in, Obama unceremoniously dumped Jane Dystel as his agent for Robert Barnett, the powerful Washington lawyer who has represented the Clintons and a host of other major Washington political figures.

Why? Cold cash. Agents take a flat percentage of all the clients' earnings, usually 15 percent. Barnett charges by the hour, which means that the bill is substantially smaller as a portion of the proceeds on big deals. Jane Dystel was furious. Obama didn't care. *The Audacity of Hope* sold 67,000 copies in its first week.

Screw you, Jane, old friend.

Obama the Cold. It's all about power.

Whack!

Then there was the Illinois State Senate Race. It proves that Obama fully understood the old Chicago saying, "Politics ain't beanbag."

In his first race for office, seeking a state Senate seat on Chicago's gritty South Side in 1996, Obama cleverly used election rules to invalidate the voting petition signatures of four competitors, including those of his former mentor Alice Palmer, the incumbent.

It was a slick trick. Palmer decided to not run for re-election to her state Senate seat and run instead to fill the vacated 2nd District congressional seat left open by the resignation of Rep. Mel Reynolds, convicted on sex charges. Palmer hand-picked Barack Obama to be her successor.

In the 1996 special primary election to replace Reynolds, Palmer came in a distant third behind Jesse Jackson, Jr. After her defeat, Palmer decided to keep her State Senate seat and ran for re-election against Obama. She filed nominating petitions with 1,580 signatures on December 18, 1995—the last day to file nominating petitions.

That annoyed Barack Obama. As a community organizer and manager of Project Vote, had helped register thousands of voters and knew Chicago rules to the letter. He challenged Palmer's hastily gathered nominating petitions and those of the three other prospective Democratic primary candidates.

Nearly two-thirds of Palmer's signatures were found to be invalid, leaving her almost 200 signatures short of the required 757 signatures of registered voters residing in the Senate district; none of the other three prospective candidates had the required number of valid signatures, leaving Obama, who had filed nominating petitions with over 3,000 signatures on the first filing day, as the only candidate to earn a place on the March 1996 Democratic primary ballot.

The Chicago Tribune asked Obama if voters were not disserviced by a ballot with no opposing candidates, and Obama said "I think they ended up with a very good state senator."

John Kass, a veteran *Chicago Tribune* columnist, commented during the 2008 presidential race, "Knock out your opposition, challenge their petitions, destroy your enemy, right? It is how Barack Obama destroyed his enemies back in 1996 that conflicts with his message today."

Doing the community organizer grunt work of registering Chicago voters means you know all the rules, including how to get enough valid signatures to stay in the race and keep your enemies out.

Screw you, Alice, old friend.

Obama the Cold. It's all about power.

Whack!

Obama the Cold is the real man issuing all those game-changing Executive Orders.

Now, what about that Executive Order on Environmental Leadership? What does it mean exactly?

If you read the whole fifteen-page E.O., you see that there's much more to it than reported in the *Washington Post*'s article, "Agencies Told to Reduce Emissions."

There's even much more to it than advertised in the official White House news release we saw earlier, "To require Federal agencies to set a 2020 greenhouse gas emissions reduction target; increase energy efficiency; reduce fleet petroleum consumption; conserve water; reduce waste; support sustainable communities; and leverage Federal purchasing power to promote environmentally-responsible products and technologies."

The devil is in the details. It fact there are enough detail to make this E.O. look like Dante's *Inferno*. Buried on Page 12, deep in the E.O., inside a paragraph titled, "Agency Roles in Support of Federal Adaptation Strategy," are these instructions:

> The agencies shall participate actively in the interagency Climate Change Adaptation Task Force, which is already engaged in developing the domestic and international dimensions of a U.S. strategy for adaptation to climate change, and shall develop approaches through which the policies and practices of the agencies can be made compatible with and reinforce that strategy.

That word "Adaptation" is a red flag to insiders. It's the new Washington-speak buzzword meaning, "Let's grab total control of America's economy and society by claiming we're saving them from climate doom."

The "Climate Change Adaptation Task Force" was quietly created in mid-2009 by the White House Council on Environmental Quality (CEQ). It initially involved 23 federal agencies, departments, and offices to decide what the government will do to "adapt" to climate change – accepting without question the supposedly "settled science" that global warming was not only real, but also caused entirely by human activity.

What's remarkable is that nobody in the media noticed that Obama's "adaptation task force" concept was lifted bodily from the 684-page House cap-and-trade bill, H.R. 2454, "the American Clean Energy and Security Act," co-sponsored in May by Reps. Henry Waxman (D-CA) and Edward Markey (D-MA).

Buried deep inside that bill, Section 472 would create a "Climate Change Adaptation Panel" comprised of every federal agency head with responsibility for some part of America's natural resources – the same 23 "panel" executives as in the CEQ "task force," ranging from the heads of the national forests and national parks to the Army Corps of Engineers and the National Oceanic and Atmospheric Administration (NOAA).

This panel of "Deputy Climate Czars" would be chaired by the head of the President's Council on Environmental Quality (CEQ), Nancy Sutley. The House bill instructed the panel to come up with a "Natural Resources Climate Change Adaptation Strategy" that would make climate change *each agency's highest priority,* just exactly what Obama's E.O. did in October that Congress couldn't do in May.

The speed with which the bureaucrats responded to Obama's Executive Order was head-spinning. Here's just one example of what really happened in 23 federal departments:

Interior Secretary Ken Salazar created a "climate change response council" to coordinate the department's eight bureaus and offices, including the Fish and Wildlife Service.

The U.S. Fish and Wildlife Service (FWS) is a lot more important to America's daily life than it might appear: it's the law enforcement agency for the Endangered Species Act, which has power far beyond anything the public is aware of.

For example, in February 1993 the FWS arrested Taiwanese immigrant farmer Taung Ming-Lin near Bakersfield, California for "disturbing habitat" of five Tipton kangaroo rats while his farmhands plowed his own field. Even his *tractor* was chained up and hauled to court. Facing heavy fines and three years in prison, Taung accepted a plea bargain, paid a $5,000 penalty, and agreed to get permits from several agencies before plowing his own land again.

Did Taung kill five rats? No. He "disturbed" the dirt in his own field that they supposedly lived in.

As many critics have pointed out, the Endangered Species Act is not an animal and plant protection law, it is a federal *land control* law: its main job is to protect *habitat* from human disturbance any place it may be found, *including private property*.

The Endangered Species Act trumps your property rights – and everybody else's.

The penalties for disturbing "critical habitat" on your own property are draconian. Cutting your own brush that might be used at some future time for nesting by an endangered bird can bring a $50,000 fine and a one year felony sentence in federal prison per incident.

And that was before the new policy of making climate change "adaptation" the *highest priority,* completely changing the mission of the bulk of America's bureaucracy.

It doesn't take much imagination to see what impact Obama's Adaptation policy could have on America's most fundamental right – to own and enjoy private property.

Now that we understand the vast power of the Fish and Wildlife Service, what really happened?

The U.S. Fish and Wildlife Service under Secretary Ken Salazar is run by up-through-the-ranks veteran Sam Hamilton. It is a big agency with nearly 8,000 employees and a $2.3 billion budget (2008) that manages a large number of hunting and fishing opportunities – its units include the Federal Duck Stamp and National Fish Hatchery programs, as well as the Migratory Birds and Endangered Species programs.

One of FWS's star projects is the National Wildlife Refuge System (NWRS) – 550 national wildlife refuges and 37 wetland management districts covering more than 150 million acres. That's a lot of territory.

Not many people besides hunters and anglers know this, but the refuge system also manages six wildlife-dependent *recreational uses,* topped by hunting and fishing.

Hunting and fishing in national wildlife refuges? Many Americans find that a contradiction in terms, but hunting and fishing license fees have supported the refuges since predecessor agencies were established in the 19th Century. As the NWRS website says:

> Hunters get a warm welcome at more than 300 hunting programs on refuges and on about 36,000 Waterfowl Production Areas. Opportunities for fresh or saltwater fishing are available at more than 270 refuges. There is at least one wildlife refuge in every state and one within an hour's drive of most major cities.

Nearly 40 million people visit national wildlife refuges each year. The $1.7 billion in sales they generate for regional economies supports about 27,000 jobs and $542.8 million in employment income.

Hamilton's staff released the U.S. Fish and Wildlife Service's "proposed Strategic Plan for Climate Change" in late September, 2009 with this notice:

> Climate change must become our highest priority. Consequently, we will deploy our resources, creativity and energy in a long-term campaign to reduce greenhouse gas emissions and safeguard fish, wildlife and their habitats.

> The proposed Action Plan for Climate Change, an appendix to the Strategic Plan, details the specific actions the Service will take during the next five years to implement the Strategic Plan.

Neither the proposed FWS Strategic Plan nor its detailed Action Plan even mentions the words "hunting" or "fishing." It was not an oversight. Green pressure groups want them gone.

For example, the new FWS Climate Change web page links directly to a page titled, "Season's End: Global Warming's Threat to Hunting and Fishing." You have to look carefully to realize that you have left the official FWS website for a private environmental group's propaganda.

"Season's End" paints a grim picture of ruined habitat, species extinction, refuge closures, visitor shut-outs, travel restrictions, and general gloom, to be prevented only by adoption of "a robust answer to the threat of climate change," which includes "preventing the worst impacts and preparing for the reality that global warming impacts are already occurring."

In other words, vote for the Climate Change bill in order to fund federal programs "preventing the worst impacts" – and *maybe* keep the refuges open for hunting and fishing, which otherwise might not happen. The political message is not subtle, and looks like it's from a government agency, but it's from the so-called "Bi-Partisan Policy Center," a private group supported by $16 million in grants from The Energy Foundation, the Hewlett Foundation, the Pew Charitable Trusts, and the Joyce Foundation, none of which is known for vigorous endorsement of hunting and fishing. In fact, during the 1980s and '90s, the Joyce Foundation was the nation's premier funder of gun control organizations.

The environmental movement's climate faction has gained control of America's bureaucracy through pressure on the

Obama Administration which resulted in the Executive Order on climate change.

So, what does the Executive Order's long list of generalities mean, exactly?

It means that all the agencies in the federal government must make climate change their highest priority, regardless what Congress has ever instructed them to do – the law changed by Executive Order.

It means that the instruction to "reduce fleet petroleum consumption" goes far beyond making government vehicles use alternative fuels, it means that all agencies that control access permits on federal land must consider climate change before they consider the nation's energy needs – the bureaucrats who issue permits to mine coal or drill for oil and natural gas on government lands immediately began erecting barriers to producers who fuel American's entire economy.

That's a game changer.

All because people have been led to believe in "man-made global warming," and that "the science is settled," and cannot be questioned.

Then on November 20, 2009, the game changer got changed.

A computer used by the Climatic Research Unit (CRU) of the University of East Anglia (UEA) in Norwich, England, suffered a disaster: Someone released thousands of e-mails and documents from its server. It was 4,000 files created by the world's leading climate scientists, and showed that they had been systematically and persistently withholding scientific information, interfering with the peer-review process of scientific papers, deleting information to prevent disclosure under the United Kingdom's Freedom of Information Act, and selecting only data that supported the case for global warming.

London headlines blared, "Climate scientists accused of 'manipulating global warming data'" (*Daily Telegraph*) and "Climate skeptics claim leaked emails are evidence of collusion among scientists." (*The Guardian*). "Skeptics publish climate e-mails 'stolen from East Anglia University'" (*The Times*).

Climate believers frantically denied that the stunning revelations cast any doubt on manmade global warming. Climate skeptics said they did. A British blogger named James Delingpole dubbed the scandal "Climategate." The name stuck.

At the very least, the world now knew that a few "gatekeeper" scientists at the highest levels had kept opposing views out of scientific journals; so a substantial fraction of climate science never got published because it disagreed with the "gatekeepers."

Public interest in global warming fell to ho-hum levels.

The Climategate files were first uploaded by a computer in Turkey to the RealClimate website, used by climate scientists to explain their work, but Gavin Schmidt, co-founder of the site saw it 25 minutes later and shut the site down so nobody could see it. Then a computer in Saudi Arabia uploaded the files to an anonymous-forwarding server in Tomsk, Russian Federation and sent a link to The Air Vent website used by opposing scientists. From there it was picked up by hundreds of blogs and news services around the world.

I checked with several experts who had read and analyzed the emails and listened to their views about who hacked them and why. Scotland Yard in England was treating it as a criminal theft, although nothing was actually erased and removed from CRU computers, it was merely copied and released. It was the secret *knowledge* that had been "stolen."

But there was something odd about what the experts told me: it was all so tidy.

The emails contained nothing but technical discussions, all on topic, no gossip, no personal matters, no day-to-day let's-have-a-pint-after-work chit-chat that you'd normally find mixed in with even the most geeky scientist's messages, all as if they'd been sorted carefully.

Same with the documents and data codes, nothing random, no sign of simply rummaging through the computer for data mining, just careful sorting.

That was too curious. So I went to one of many download sites that had sprung up around the world and downloaded the infamous Climategate files.

I was astounded at what I saw. All 4,000 documents were in one zip file folder titled FOI. That stands for Freedom of Information in the U.K., just as it does in the U.S. The main folder had two subfolders, one titled Email, the other titled

Documents. Very tidy.

What I was looking at appeared to be an inside job by a disaffected colleague, but the University of East Anglia said that was highly unlikely.

Well, with messages from senior scientists saying, "Don't tell Smith there's a Freedom of Information Act in the U.K." it wouldn't be too hard to get disaffected with CRU "gatekeepers."

Climategate perpetrators and their colleagues said the revelations weren't a gamechanger.

But two weeks later Senate Majority Leader Harry Reid put his climate change bill on the backburner, saying they'd take it up later. Game change.

Then came the much anticipated Copenhagen Climate Conference, where a legally binding limit on greenhouse gas emissions would be forged and huge transfer payments from the developed countries to developing countries would be mandated.

Politicians said the Climategate revelations wouldn't stop a binding agreement.

Obama and a lot of junketing congressmen went to Copenhagen and came back without a binding agreement. Game change.

Then in January of 2010, the White House Council on Environmental Quality disabled their Climate Change Adaptation Task Force web page and removed the term from the White House search engine. Game change.

Even the Washington Post gave the world's leading climate skeptic, Bjorn Lomborg, a bully pulpit with his opinion piece, "From Copenhagen's ashes, a better way to fight global warming," which carried this intelligent, common-sense message:

> Given that global energy demand is expected to double by 2050, the only way to reduce (if not eliminate) our use of fossil fuels without crippling the world economy is to radically ramp up green-energy technologies – to the point where we can increase our reliance on them by several orders of magnitude. For two decades we have been putting the cart before the horse, pretending that we could cut carbon emissions now and

> solve the technology problem later. It's time to turn things around. Instead of condemning billions of people to continued poverty by trying to make fossil fuels more expensive, we should make green energy cheaper. This means radically increasing spending on research and development.

Game change. It took a big dose of truth about the climate change mafia to make the Chicago White House mafia back off a little from an arguably unconstitutional mission change for the entire American executive apparatus.

But taking a web page down doesn't mean the mission change is gone. Climate change adaptation is still the highest priority on the Fish and Wildlife website, and remains in force in the other federal agencies.

So President Barack Obama and his Democrat Congress, although shaken by the loss of Ted Kennedy's Senate seat to Republican Scott Brown, are still beating the United States Constitution black and blue.

Their pressure group buddies will ramp up their demands, not lessen them. They'll have to retreat and rely more on regulations like the climate change Executive Order. But they won't go away. Ever. In politics, it's never over.

We mustn't forget that fairly routine Tuesday morning at the White House when CNBC correspondent John Harwood sat conducting an interview with President Barack Obama – and the fly came by.

It's still just as symbolic of Barack Obama – and his Democrat Congress, too. That's what they're doing to the United States Constitution, the "deeply flawed" document Professor Obama taught at the University of Chicago.

Whacking it dead and brushing it off onto the floor.

Screw you, America, old friend.

Obama the Cold. It's all about power.

Whack!